Behaviorism

Interpretations

series editor: Roy Harris

This new series aims to explore the key concepts of intellectual enquiry in the Western world. Some of these concepts have a long and controversial history; others are of relatively recent origin. All are open to different interpretations by different thinkers.

Interpretations has two main aims:

to offer a survey of the main interpretations of an idea: those interpretations which have been influential in the history of Western thought

to offer experts an opportunity to present their own interpretation both of the idea and of its historical importance.

While giving the student an introduction to an important topic in the history of ideas, each volume in the series also represents an original contribution to that subject by a specialist in the field.

The language of the series is that of the general reader. All unfamiliar or technical terms are fully explained and critically evaluated.

Behaviorism

Mind, Mechanism and Society

John Staddon

Duckworth

First published in 1993 by
Gerald Duckworth & Co. Ltd.
The Old Piano Factory
48 Hoxton Square, London N1 6PB
Tel: 071 729 5986
Fax: 071 729 0015

Distributed in USA by
Focus Information Group
PO Box 369
Newburyport, MA 01950

A catalogue record for this book is available
from the British Library

ISBN 0 7156 2488 1

Typeset by Ray Davies
Printed in Great Britain by
Redwood Books, Trowbridge, Wiltshire

Contents

To Lucinda

Preface

I never used to think of myself as a behaviorist, but now I see that I have been ignoring the evidence. Graduate research in the Harvard 'pigeon lab'; a career of experimental work on learning, largely with animals; a distrust of partitions of the mind into cognitive and noncognitive bits: the data are clear, the behavioristic signs unmistakable. I failed to recognize them because I have never found the atheoretical simplism of Skinnerian behaviorism appealing, and the theoretical efforts of the Hullian behaviorists always struck me as clumsy and prematurely physiological. But dissatisfaction with your family doesn't mean that you don't belong to it. When Professor Harris asked me to write this book, I was happy to comply because I had been thinking informally about these issues for some time, without any clear plan as to what to do with my ideas.

The book is a short intellectual history of behaviorism and a proposal for a new theoretical behaviorism. The history emphasizes Skinnerian radical behaviorism, because it still survives as a coherent movement and has had the greatest popular impact. The new theoretical behaviorism isn't really an '-ism' at all, but a framework for scientific psychology that will, I hope, achieve general acceptance.

I am immensely grateful to the friends and colleagues who read early drafts of the book and saved me from my most egregious errors (no doubt subtler errors remain). I particularly thank Nancy Innis, Gregory Kimble, Armando Machado and Clive Wynne. I also thank Roy Harris for his timely invitation to contribute to this series. I am grateful to the US National Science Foundation and National Institutes of Mental Health for research support over many years.

Durham, North Carolina   J.S.

1

Early Behaviorism

Will Rogers, the American humorist, is reported to have identi-fied his political allegiances by saying 'I am not member of any organized political group. I am a Democrat.' If he'd been a psychologist, he might have said: 'I am not in any organized discipline. I am a psychologist.' If Psychology is a field it is a field of battle, where contending groups struggle for mastery – not a coherent discipline.

Many eminent psychologists, beginning with William James, have tried to sort out the divisions within Psychology. James's suggestion, before the advent of behaviorism, was to divide psychologists into 'tough-' and 'tender-minded'. He might also have mentioned the division between practice (clinical psycho-logy) and basic research (experimental psychology), between 'social-science' and 'natural-science', or between 'structural' and 'functional' approaches – not to mention the split between mentalists and realists. The nineteenth-century ancestor of the mentalists is Gustav Fechner, 'father' of psychophysics. Fech-ner was the co-discoverer of the Weber-Fechner law, which relates the magnitude of a 'sensation' to the magnitude of the physical stimulus. He believed in a mental realm with concepts and measurements that owe nothing to biology. Many contem-porary cognitive psychologists agree with him. On the other side are biological psychologists, who believe that the fact of Darwin-ian evolution means that the behavior of people and non-human animals has common roots and must therefore share important properties.[1]

Since the advent of behaviorism in the early part of this century, it has been a reference point for doctrinal debates in psychology. Even today, many scholarly papers in cognitive psychology either begin or end with a ritual paragraph of behaviorist-bashing – pointing out how this or that version of behavioristic theory is completely unable to handle this or that experimental finding or property that mind 'must' possess. Theoretical positions are almost always identified by their opposition to behaviorism. Much 'cognitive' theory is perfectly behavioristic, but the 'cognitive' banner is proudly born. Few theorists want to be mistaken for behaviorists.

The behaviorists, in their turn, often protect their turf by concocting a forbidding jargon and insisting on conceptual and linguistic purity in those who would publish in their journals. Theories, if entertained at all, are required to meet stringent, not always well-defined and sometimes impossible criteria. The behaviorists have not always served their cause well.

In recent years, behaviorism has been on the retreat within psychology. In 1989 a leading neo-behaviorist could write, 'I have ... used a parliamentary metaphor to characterize the confrontation ... between those who have taken a stimulus-response (S-R) behavioristic approach and those who favor a cognitive approach ... and I like to point out that the S-R psychologists, who at one time formed the government, are now in the loyal opposition ...'[2] Most recently, in a turnabout comment on J.S. Kennedy's behavioristically oriented book *The New Anthropomorphism* a reviewer wrote: 'If anthropomorphism produces results that are, in the normal manner of science, valuable, it will be persisted with; if it does not, it will be abandoned. It was, after all, abandoned once before. The only danger ... is that scientists can be enduringly obstinate in their investigations of blind alleys. Just think how long behaviourism lasted in psychology.'[3]

Behaviorism is frequently declared dead. But although services are held regularly, the corpse keeps creeping out of the coffin. The disinterested observer might well conclude that vigorous attacks on an allegedly moribund movement are a signal that behaviorism threatens to resurrect. Indeed it does.

The origins of behaviorism

So what is behaviorism, and how did it begin? The word was coined by Johns Hopkins psychologist John Broadus Watson (1878-1958) in a nineteen-page article in the theoretical journal *Psychological Review*[4] in 1913. Over the next few years, Watson followed up with several books advocating behaviorism. He was reacting against the doctrine of *introspection*, the idea that the basic data of psychology could be gathered from one's own consciousness or the inferred consciousness of others. Emigré German behaviorist Max Meyer made this distinction between private and public events explicit in a later work, *Psychology of the other one.*[5]

Box 1.1

Psychology as the behaviorist views it is a purely objective experimental branch of natural science. Its theoretical goal is the prediction and control of behavior. Introspection forms no essential part of its methods, nor is the scientific value of its data dependent upon the readiness with which they lend themselves to interpretation in terms of consciousness. The behaviorist, in his efforts to get a unitary scheme of animal response, recognizes no dividing line between man and brute. (John Broadus Watson[6])

Behaviorists of nearly all varieties, early as well as contemporary, agree on the following reasoning: psychology is a science; and because it is a science, its data are *public*. Physicist John Ziman[7] much later popularized this idea and used it as a definition of all science, which he called 'public knowledge'. The idea of *objectivity*, defined in terms of consensual agreement among external observers, was emphasized most strongly by the Vienna Circle positivists, but had its origins much earlier and was very much in the air as Watson wrote his first paper. Behaviorism (for Watson) is just the redefinition of psychology as the objective study of behavior (see Box 1.1).

Obviously introspective feelings, visions and images – what you or I feel or see in our 'mind's eye' – are not public in Ziman's sense. The subjective aspects of consciousness, therefore (according to Watson and Meyer), cannot be the subject matter of a science. It is interesting that this issue is still a contentious one. For example, British physicist Brian Pippard recently wrote in the leading scientific weekly *Nature*: 'All too rarely do I find colleagues who will assent to the proposition (which I find irresistible) that the very ground-rules of science, its concern only for public knowledge, preclude its finding an explanation for my consciousness, the one phenomenon of which I am absolutely certain.[8] Since psychology was at one time defined as the study of consciousness, and since the so-called 'cognitive revolution' has once more legitimized speculation about consciousness and theories derived from intuitions about consciousness, it is obvious why behaviorism is a source of controversy in present-day psychology (more about consciousness in Chapter 5).

My consciousness (or yours) is revealed to others through *speech*, of course. And my speech (as opposed to the *meaning* of my speech) *is* public. Since Watson, behaviorists have been very happy to take language (renamed 'verbal behavior') as one of their domains.

So far I have described what has come to be known as *methodological* behaviorism, which asserts little with which any general experimental psychologist would disagree. But Watson went well beyond insistence on objectivity and 'the other one' to argue against any kind of theory that did not explicitly refer to observables, either 'real' observables, or things like 'covert responses' that sound like observables, even if they cannot be measured directly. Thus *thought*, for Watson, was nothing but 'covert speech' measurable, perhaps, by imperceptible movements of the vocal chords. Other aspects of consciousness were similarly reduced to muscular movements or the perception of such movements. This emphasis drew the attention of experimenters to many hitherto unexpected physiological accompaniments of conscious experience, such as 'rapid-eye-movement' (REM) sleep as a signal of dreaming, or the direction of gaze as an indicator of the contents of thought. But it was theoretically much less productive. Watson's preoccupation with the sensations of movement left a legacy of obsession with *proprioception* that was to constrict behavioristic theorizing for decades.

Behaviorism and learning. The behaviorist emphasis on the forces that change behavior has meant that behaviorism, as an approach to psychology, is almost coextensive with the psychological study of *learning*, particularly learning in animals.[9] A history of behaviorism features many of the same stars as a history of learning psychology.

The behaviorist movement was strongly influenced by the studies of *conditioned reflexes* by the Russian physiologists

1. Early Behaviorism

Pavlov, Bekhterev and their associates. Ivan P. Pavlov (1849-1936) was a gastric physiologist. He ran a large institute in the Military Medical Academy in St Petersburg from 1895 for many years. In 1904 Pavlov won a Nobel Prize for his contributions to gastric physiology, but he is of course much better known for his work on what he called 'psychic secretions' – the salivation of dogs in response to a bell, a tone or some other neutral stimulus that has been reliably paired with the presentation of food.

Since René Descartes in the seventeenth century, physiologists and psychologists had been familiar with the idea of the *reflex*, the inborn almost automatic elicitation of a response, such as an eyeblink, by a suitable stimulus, such as a puff of air to the eye. This apparently simple phenomenon, so similar to the intuitive idea of cause and effect, was very attractive to Cartesians, concerned to understand behavior in mechanical terms. But *learning* always posed something of a problem, because as an organism learns, previously ineffective stimuli become effective and previously effective stimuli may cease to be effective. Pavlov's conditioned reflex, in which a neutral stimulus acquires the power to elicit a response, seemed to resolve this contradiction. Here was an apparently mechanical process that nevertheless allowed stimuli to have different effects at different times. The reflex model could be preserved, but learning could be accommodated.

As experimental work progressed in the twentieth century, it became increasingly obvious that Pavlovian or *classical* conditioning is in fact a rather poor model for much of what humans and animals do. Instrumental or *operant* conditioning (about which more in a moment) provides a much better model, but at the cost of abandoning the simple cause-effect, stimulus-response (S-R) behavioral building block.

But none of this was apparent in the early part of the twentieth century, when Watson first saw the potential of Pavlovian experiments and analyses. Under the Pavlovian influence, Watson placed a heavy emphasis on stimulus-response learning. Despite, or perhaps because of his early experience studying the instinctive behavior of seabirds – terns – on the Dry Tortuga islands in the Florida Keys, Watson thought that most human behavior is not instinctive. Nevertheless, his biological training had given him faith in the essential simplicity of all behavior. He therefore believed human behavior, despite its apparent complexity, to be basically unmysterious and comprehensible. Seeking a simple alternative to instinct, he hit upon stimulus-response learning, exemplified by Pavlovian experiments, as a suitably plastic means for the development of adaptive behavior during the lifetime of the individual. Since the mechanism of stimulus-response learning was presumed to be both uniform and well understood, Watson's view gave priority to the environment as a determiner of behavior. Nurture, not nature was the key. This emphasis on the environment has been a continuing theme in the varieties of behaviorism that grew out of Watson's original proposal.

In addition to the Pavlovian and positivistic influences, Watson's approach to psychology also derived from biologist Jacques Loeb (1859-1924), who was one of his teachers at Chicago. Loeb was a Jewish-intellectual emigré from Germany who came to the US to escape from discrimination in his native country. Loeb did well in the US, spending most of his career at the University of Chicago. His work at that time was with invertebrates and plants and, as might be expected, he found their behavior to be relatively simple. He invented a theory of what he called *tropisms*, which were simple orienting mechanisms that allowed these primitive organisms to approach or avoid light, find food or a mate and so on. Watson's own interests were in human behavior and in learning, which could not easily be handled by tropisms in the Loeb style – hence Watson's fascination with conditioning. Nevertheless, he took from Loeb a preference for simple, mechanistic explanations. A good idea, in principle. Unfortunately, Watson's idea of 'simple' was probably too simple and, as I will show in more detail in Chapter 5, the idea of 'mechanism' to which old-style behaviorism has led now appears to be unworkable.

Watson left Chicago for a professorship at the new Johns Hopkins University in Baltimore. Unfortunately, his promising career was cut short after a few years by a scandal – an adulterous affair with a graduate student whom he subsequently married. As a result, Watson left academic life for a successful career in advertising. His success in this new field was no accident. The major figures in the softer sciences have almost invariably been people whose chief talent is in *rhetoric*, the art of verbal persuasion. They may have other skills (Skinner was a brilliant experimenter, for example), but their ability to found schools usually owes at least as much to their ability to persuade and organize as to their experimental and theoretical talents. Some examples in a moment.

The next generation

Watson's target was the target of all psychologists: human behavior. But his disavowal of consciousness, his inability to cope with the complexities of verbal behavior, and his training as a biologist, meant that the immediate experimental future of behaviorism lay with animal experiments.

Psychological work with animals had already been pioneered by Edward L. Thorndike (1874-1949) at Harvard and then at Columbia University. In his doctoral thesis, Thorndike studied the behavior of cats escaping from puzzle boxes. The animal had to push a pole or pull a chain to allow it to get out and eat a little food. Thorndike discovered that his cats seemed to learn this task in a rather simple way. At first they behaved more or less randomly, pushing the pole at first by accident. But then they would tend to repeat on the next trial exactly the behavior that had been followed by reward on the previous trial. Thorndike summarized his observations in what he called the *Law of Effect* (see Box 1.2). The Law of Effect formed the basis for the development of *reinforcement theory*, which has been the main theoretical preoccupation of the behaviorist movement. Following the lead of Thorndike and Watson, the next generation of behaviorists were the founders of the 'rat psychology' that was to dominate the American academic scene for the next several decades.

Box 1.2. The Law of Effect

Of several responses made to the same situation, those which are accompanied or closely followed by satisfaction to the animal ... will, other things being equal, be more firmly connected with the situation ...; those which are accompanied or closely followed by discomfort ... will have their connections with the situation weakened ... The greater the satisfaction or discomfort, the greater the strengthening or weakening of the bond. (Edward L. Thorndike[10])

The three names usually associated with the rat psychology of the thirties, forties and fifties are Guthrie, Hull and Tolman. However, Watson's real heir was B.F. Skinner, who rose to prominence a little later. Skinner invented new experimental methods for studying learning in animals. On the philosophical front, he applied behavioristic ideas to every aspect of human experience, including consciousness. Skinner's *radical behaviorism* is Watson's most enduring legacy. Because of Skinner's influence, and his willingness to speculate about every aspect of human experience, his work is the main topic of this book. But the context, and the mainstream of behavioral psychology, was set by Hull and Tolman, to whose work I turn next.

Watson was one of the first to put rats through mazes, but the technique was exploited most extensively by Yale psychologist Clark L. Hull (1884-1952) and his followers, most notably his chief disciple Kenneth Spence. Hull was a late developer in psychology, but in middle years he became acquainted with the theory of physics, in its classical, Newtonian form, and his major contribution to the field was a treatise, *The principles of behavior*,[11] in which he proposed a cumbersome mathematical formulation to explain learning in the white rat. Hull was a catalyst rather than a great teacher. His weekly seminars at Yale became famous, and his ideas were spread by those who attended them to many other universities across the United States. But his most prominent followers were supervised by others, and few of his own students made names in academic psychology.

Hull's experimental method is still the norm in much of psychology. Groups of subjects are exposed to different conditions of reward (rats running down a straight runway to food pellets of different sizes, for example). The performances of the individuals (e.g. their running speeds) are then averaged and compared statistically to see if the independent variable (the thing varied among groups, pellet size, for example) has an effect. The method, as a way of understanding processes that take place in individuals rather than in the group, rests on assumptions about the essential uniformity of the subjects that were not understood for many years. Indeed, the limitations of what has come to be termed *between-group* methodology are yet to be grasped fully by the psychological community. (The limitations of the competing, within-animal method, are also not widely understood, as we will see shortly.)

Box 1.3. The Varieties of Behaviorism

CLASSICAL: The behaviorism of Watson; the objective study of behavior; no mental life, no internal states; thought is covert speech.

METHODOLOGICAL: The objective study of third-person behavior; the data of psychology must be intersubjectively verifiable; no theoretical prescriptions. Has been absorbed into general experimental and cognitive psychology.

NEO-: Hullian and post-Hullian, theoretical, group data, not dynamic.

RADICAL: Skinnerian behaviorism; includes behavioral approach to 'mental life'; not mechanistic; internal states not permitted.

TELEOLOGICAL: Post-Skinnerian, purposive, close to microeconomics.

THEORETICAL: Post-Skinnerian, accepts internal states (the skin makes a difference); dynamic, but eclectic in choice of theoretical structures.

Like all the early behaviorists (see Box 1.3), Hull was a philosophical descendant of the British Empiricists, Locke, Berkeley and Hume, and inherited their belief in *associations* as the primary psychological unit. He was for a while much taken with the philosophical position *logical positivism*. He had earlier been influenced by Isaac Newton's *Principia mathematica*. The latter two influences led him to prefer a mathematical, highly formal approach to theory, despite his own quite limited mathematical capabilities. Like Skinner and many other American scientists in the Edison tradition, he was a gifted gadgeteer; but unlike Skinner, he admired abstract theory more than practical machinery.

It is helpful to organize the theoretical ideas of Hull and Tolman in terms of three questions: What *data* did they attempt to explain? Where did their theoretical *concepts* come from? What *form* did their theories take?

Explanation: Hull. Clark Hull was interested in explaining data from experiments with rats learning simple maze tasks under the action of food reward and with people learning to recall lists of nonsense syllables (i.e. trigrams such as JIV that do not correspond to actual words) under verbal instructions. The data to be explained were not so much the details of moment-by-moment behavior of individuals as 'functional relations' based on data from groups of subjects. For example, the negatively accelerated *learning curve* that relates some measure (several were used) of performance on a learning task to learning trials: percentage of correct responses in a two-choice task, for example, typically increases rapidly at first, then more slowly later as it approaches 100 per cent. Another standard function was the *delay-of-reinforcement gradient*, which showed how performance declines as the time between the reinforced response and the reinforcement is increased.

Hull's theoretical concepts came from an associationist view of the causal chain between stimulus and response and a Watsonian notion of 'ideas' as manifestations of overt or covert motor activity. Each 'response' was characterized by a final 'strength', called by Hull *reaction potential*, which was in turn determined by intervening variables (the latter term is from Tolman, about whom more in a moment) such as *habit strength* and *generalization*. The variability characteristic of behavior was accommodated by the assumption of *behavioral oscillation* of reaction potential – what would now be termed a *stochastic* (variable-in-time) process. Each of these intervening variables was assumed to be linked in some way to observables. Experimental results were deduced formally as predictions from this rather lumbering system.

Some of Hull's theoretical elements were drawn from Pavlov, many of whose own ideas were based on his conjectures about brain function. The basic 'glue' that allowed learning to occur was assumed to be Pavlovian conditioning, conceived of as a process by which stimulus and response become causally linked. This usage (which has become standard among Hull's intellectual descendants) goes well beyond Pavlov. For Pavlov, the term 'conditional' was largely descriptive, implying nothing more than the observation that elicitation of salivation (the *conditioned response*: CR) by the tone (*conditioned stimulus*: CS) is conditional upon pairing between the CS and the *unconditioned stimulus* (US), food (see Fig. 1.1). But for the Hullians, the process that underlies Pavlovian conditioning was a theoretical atom, which could then be used to explain more complex behavior. *Generalization*, the idea that training with one stimulus and response will increase the tendency to respond to similar stimuli and to make similar responses, was another idea from Pavlov. Other ideas came from Sherringtonian[12] reflexology: for example, the idea of *reception*, a process modelled on what was then known of receptor physiology; the idea of *interaction* between stimulus effects (added to accommodate 'whole-greater-than-sum-of-parts' effects made famous by the German *Gestalt* ['form'] psychologists); and the idea of a stimulus *trace* that persists after the physical stimulus has ceased.

Pavlovian Conditioning Procedures

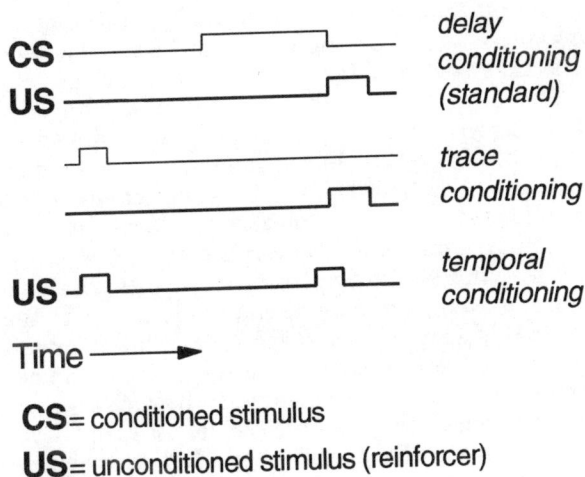

CS — delay conditioning (standard)
US —

trace conditioning

US — temporal conditioning

Time ⟶

CS = conditioned stimulus

US = unconditioned stimulus (reinforcer)

Fig. 1.1. Time relations between conditioned stimulus (e.g. a tone, CS: light lines) and unconditioned stimulus (e.g. food, US: heavy lines) in some Pavlovian conditioning procedures. In delay conditioning, for example, after one of these pairings has been repeated a sufficient number of times, the response reliably made to the unconditioned stimulus (e.g. salivation) comes to occur when the CS is presented. (When the response – salivation – occurs to the CS, it is called the conditioned response: CR.) In trace conditioning, the CR usually occurs after the CS, and close to the time when the US will occur. In temporal conditioning each US presentation is the effective CS for the next US.

How were these ideas put together to explain maze learning? A detailed exposition would take us well beyond the confines of a short survey – and is in any case of largely historical interest. But some of the basic ideas can be conveyed simply. Hull tied *reinforcement*, the strengthening effect of reward on a response that produces it, to the reduction of physiological need. This turned out to be a hard assumption to prove: many rewarding events (money, for example) have no obvious link to physiology, and even food is effective as a reinforcer long before it has any nutritional consequences. The rat may well repeat his bar pressing after he gets the very first food pellet, long before his blood sugar or any other gross physiological measure shows any change. Moreover, the theoretical effects of reinforcing events can be described without specifying their physiological concomitants.

How did Hull conceive of the effects of reinforcement? One effect was to 'condition' (in the Pavlovian sense) events occurring at the time the 'goal' (e.g. food at the end of the maze) is reached. The basic idea was that any pair of events, A-B, that regularly occur in succession somehow become linked (just as the CS and the US become linked) so that the occurrence of A will come to call up B. This is just a physiological interpretation of Aristotle's notion of association through succession and temporal contiguity. Thus, stimuli near the goal, traces of earlier stimuli and stimuli generated by movements, or 'fractional anticipatory' movements, may become conditioned to the 'goal response'. In this way, the goal response will 'move forward' and come to occur sooner and sooner. This improvement in performance is the visible evidence that learning has occurred. Parts of this complex process were expressed quantitatively, but the details were never fully specified by Hull or by his several successors, most of whom filled in theoretical gaps as best they could with verbal arguments. Numerous flaws in the system were pointed out (see, for example, the chapter on Hull in the standard textbook on theories of learning[13]) and Hull's successors increasingly abandoned quantitative modeling. The mathematical approach was carried on largely by the so-called *mathematical learning theorists*.[14] A single very influential theoretical paper by two neo-Hullian Yale psychologists Robert Rescorla and Alan Wagner[15] has also led to several elaborations by Wagner and others.

1. Early Behaviorism

Hull's other direction was the study of verbal learning. He and several co-workers in 1940 put together an extraordinary volume describing their theory of how people learn nonsense syllables. The title of this book, *Mathematico-deductive theory of rote learning*,[16] shows its allegiance to a particular philosophy of science, and the theory was presented in a highly formal way, using the calculus of symbolic logic (Fitch, one of the book's co-authors, was a logician). Hull defended the book as follows: 'Its chief value consists in the large-scale pioneering demonstration of the logico-empirical methodology in the field of behavior' (p. xi).

To a modern reader, the 'logico-empirical methodology' with its rhetoric of mathematical theorems and corollaries, makes the work almost unreadable. Nevertheless, the assumptions of the theory are relatively simple – and important, because these ingredients, in various combinations, are part of most subsequent psychological theories. The theory explains the patterns of learning of nonsense syllables in a *serial anticipation* procedure: each syllable in a short list of 5-20 syllables is presented for a couple of seconds and the subject's task is to anticipate the next syllable. Data of interest are the patterns of errors – the so-called *serial-position effect*, which is that syllables at the beginning (primacy) and end (recency) of the list are better remembered than syllables in the middle – and the effects of the temporal spacing between list presentations (spaced vs. massed practice).

The chief theoretical ingredient is the quasi-physiological idea of a *memory trace*, left by each experienced trigram. These traces are of two kinds, excitatory and inhibitory. 'Response strength', the tendency to recall a particular syllable, is proportional to the algebraic sum of these two tendencies. A correct anticipation is presumed to occur when the summed strength exceeds a threshold, which is subject to some intrinsic variability. These ingredients, a decaying trace, excitatory and inhibitory contributions to a strength variable, stochasticity and the idea of response threshold, were to form a permanent part of the theoretical toolbox used by later learning theorists.

Most of the experiments by Hull and his students were concerned with *reinforcement learning*, that is the change in behavior observed when one or other aspect of behavior is rewarded or punished. The focus on reinforcement learning was forced by the behaviorists' experimental subject, the laboratory rat, a species poorly suited to verbal instruction. Nevertheless, the leading behaviorist in the inter-war years, Edward Chace Tolman (1886-1959), was notable for his rejection of a simple reward-and-punishment view even of rat learning. It was said of Oscar Wilde that 'His art was in his life,' because his writings are often less impressive than the anecdotes about him. Something similar may be said of Tolman. His theories now seem awkward or vague and sometimes naïve, but his openness and integrity, his eclectic approach, his personal warmth, and the inspiration he offered to numerous graduate students assure his place in the history of psychology.

Tolman's views are intermediate between Watsonian behaviorism and what is now called cognitive psychology. Indeed, apart from the fact that he worked almost exclusively with the white rat, it is not really clear why Tolman should be placed in the behaviorist camp at all. Perhaps the reason is that he identified himself as a behaviorist, albeit a *purposive* behaviorist, in his major systematic work: *Purposive behavior in animals and men*. (Perhaps another reason is that behaviorism was in effect 'the only game in town' for an experimental learning psychologist at the time when Tolman was active.) Tolman was interested in explaining data on rats finding their way through mazes of different types. He believed that rats are smart, almost as smart as people in many ways. He said in his Presidential address to the American Psychological Association that everything of importance in human psychology can be understood through the behavior of a rat at a choice point in a maze. His thinking, like his experimental subject matter, was highly spatial. He and his students devised a number of clever experiments to show that the simple stimulus-response reinforcement-learning psychology of Watson, Hull and Thorndike could not account for the spatial behavior of rats. Two examples are *latent learning* and *insight*.

Latent learning. The demonstration of learning in the apparent absence of reward – termed latent learning – was straightforward. If all learning depends on reinforcement, then hungry rats allowed to wander unfed around a novel maze should learn nothing. (A ridiculous idea, one might think, but much advance in psychology often still consists in turning common sense into scientific fact.) To test the idea, one of

Tolman's students compared the 'errors'[17] of three groups of rats: A. Rewarded (in the goal box) every time they were in the maze; B. Rewarded after two unrewarded days; and C. Rewarded only after six unrewarded days. The latent-learning group, C, soon caught up with the other groups, i.e. Group C reached the performance of Group A after only a couple of days, showing that its earlier, unrewarded experience had not been wasted. Tolman and another student, Honzik, did a similar experiment the next year and confirmed this conclusion.[18]

Argument swirled around these results. Tolman and his students contended that they reflect real unreinforced learning. One set of critics attributed the results to what would now be called 'non-cognitive' factors, such as habituation by the latent-learning group. The latent-learning group do better, these critics argued, not because they have learned anything, but because the unreinforced exposure allowed the rats to get over their fear of the novel apparatus (i.e. to *habituate*). Presumably the improvement in performance of the reinforced group must then also partly reflect habituation, which should perhaps be perceived as a component of the learning process. But the critics wished to argue that *real* learning is more than just habituation, although no proof was offered for this belief. There was also little basis for the tacit assumption that habituation itself is a primitive process.

Other critics argued that although food reinforcement was lacking in the latent-learning group, other, unspecified reinforcers might have been available (a completely unrewarded group in Tolman and Honzik's experiment nevertheless traversed the maze faster on successive days). 'Being taken out of the maze' (when a trial is over) for example, might be a reinforcer. The ad hoc invocation of reinforcers like this, no matter how plausible, makes the reinforcement-learning view invulnerable to disproof, of course, so this criticism is not acceptable.

The work of Tolman and his students soon led to an explicit distinction between *performance*, the measured change in behavior in a learning task, and *learning*, the process or processes that underlie this change. The learning-performance distinction is another commonplace: every hung-over exam-taker knows more than he can show. Learning – what the student might have done on the most searching exam under the best possible conditions – is not coextensive with his performance on this exam under these conditions. The learning-performance distinction nevertheless aroused controversy among psychologists. It was eventually accepted by most behaviorists, the single, striking exception being Skinner.

Food box

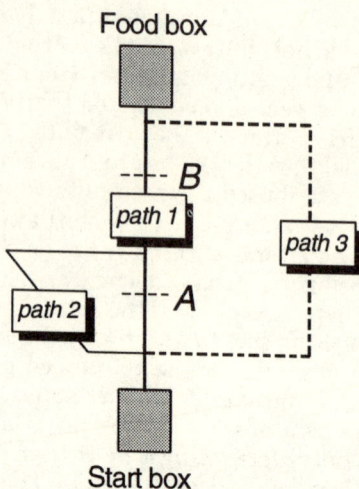

Start box

Fig. 1.2. A diagram of the maze apparatus used by Tolman and Honzik (1930). Path 1 is the shortest path from start box to food box, path 2 the next shortest and path 3 the longest. Blocks were placed at points *A* and *B* during different phases of the experiment. The question was: after encountering block *B* for the first time, will the rat pick path 2 (previously preferred to path 3, but now blocked) or path 3, the only effective route to the goal?

Insight. Tolman and Honzik[19] did another experiment, which showed that rats in some sense understand spatial constraints. Their result was cited as an example of spatial *insight*. The configuration of their maze is shown in Fig. 1.2. It allows three paths from the start box to the box where food is available. The paths differ in length: path 1 (heavy vertical line) shorter than path 2 (light line) shorter than path 3 (dashed line). In preliminary training, the rats were allowed to become familiar with all three paths to the food box and the rats had experience with a block at point *A*, which permits access to the goal only via paths 2 and 3. In the test condition, the block was moved to point *B*. Now only path 3 is open. The question is: Will the rats choose path 3 as soon as they encounter the block at *B*, or will they choose path 2 (normally preferred to path 3), indicating they do not know that paths 1 and 2 share a common, blocked, segment? Tolman and Honzik's rats acted smart, and usually went straight to path 3 after encountering the block at *B*, indicating that they knew something of the topology of the maze, and were not just operating on a fixed hierarchy of preferences. Tolman considered this behavior to be an example of 'insight', though exactly what that might mean could not be fully specified.

Explanation: Tolman. What data did Tolman attempt to explain? Where did his theoretical concepts come from? What form did his theory take? Tolman explained 'insight' behavior and latent learning by a theoretical system that drew freely on folk psychology. Tolman's rats were well supplied with 'purposes', 'expectations', and 'means-end readinesses' (loosely speaking: knowledge of what leads to what in a maze or an instrumental task). Their knowledge of the maze was represented as a *cognitive map* (a phrase now permanently associated with Tolman), which could be as rich an information store as a real map. His theoretical emphasis was almost entirely on the way in which rats represent their world. His last major paper was an attempt at what would now be called a computer simulation, although usable computers were not yet available. It is an attempt to inject *action* into this rather static theoretical picture. Cognitive maps are all very well, but a map is useless without a map *reader*, something to translate all the information into action. Later workers in the Tolman tradition did provide mechanisms to deal with some of these problems, but Tolman's chief contribution has clearly been his emphasis on what computer scientists and cognitive psychologists now term *knowledge representation*, i.e. the abstraction from reality that organisms presumably use to guide their overt behavior. This emphasis on representation was not shared by other behaviorists. It was explicitly rejected by B.F. Skinner who, like Watson, consistently opposed what he called 'structuralism.'[20]

Tolman's contemporary legacy is research on *animal cognition*, a topic that has become popular since the early 1980s.[21] Interest in spatial behavior has revived, encouraged by David Olton's introduction of a novel type of maze, the *radial-arm*

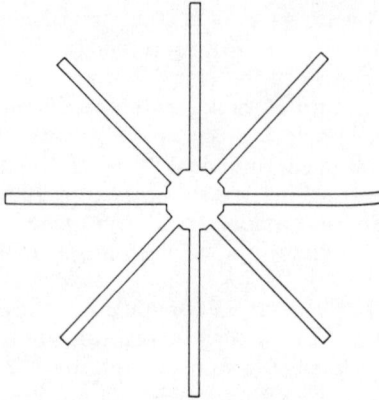

Fig. 1.3. An eight-arm radial maze. The rat begins in the center and bits of food are stored at the ends of the eight arms.

maze (Fig. 1.3). Rats in the radial-arm maze show a type of behavior unsuspected by classical reinforcement theory. At the beginning of a trial, the goal boxes at the end of the eight arms are all baited with food, and the rat is placed in the center of the maze. The rat will then visit the eight arms, usually in no particular pattern, rarely re-visiting one until all eight have been visited. (Naïve reinforcement theory would predict that the rat should return to the first rewarded arm.) Control experiments have shown that the rats use some kind of spatio-temporal representation of the maze to perform accurately. They are very accurate (i.e. rarely re-visit an arm before exploring all arms), even if interrupted after visiting four of the eight arms. If they are returned to the maze as long as an hour or more later, they nevertheless pick up where they left off and reliably select the four unvisited arms first. The radial maze has turned out to be an important tool for the investigation of memory in animals.

Another major theme in animal cognition might be termed 'Dr. Dolittle' research:[22] experiments that explore the extent to which animals can do difficult things that people can do – like talk, solve abstract problems, or form concepts. This work is not theoretically motivated, for the most part. The interest is less in how animals do these things than in the simple fact that they can do them. It is a sort of natural history, exploring the limits of what animals can do.

*

The 'classical' behaviorists Hull and Tolman were keenly interested in explaining behavior in theoretical terms. But not all behaviorists accept the conventional scientific proposition that the aim of science is to *explain* the phenomena of nature. For Watson, and B.F. Skinner, the aim was 'prediction and control', essentially unaided by theory. 'Explanation' for most scientists means 'theoretical explanation'. A good theory will usually imply prediction and control as an outcome, but many good theories fail to predict very much (they may be persuasive simply because they summarize much that is already known), or may even show that certain kinds of prediction are impossible (quantum theory is the usual example). And a theory is more than the sum of its predictions: the early version of Copernicus' heliocentric theory did not predict better that the Ptolemaic theory, and the calculations required were no easier. Nevertheless, the Copernican theory is better because it is fundamentally simpler, and because it led to more powerful theories. There is thus a purpose in theorizing that goes beyond the ability of the theory to predict.

Watson's research agenda was explicitly atheoretical, and is thus scientifically eccentric. Watson's successor, B.F. Skinner, also provided an alternative to theory which was part Baconian fact gathering and part pragmatic epistemology. In his hands this mixture turned out to be enormously influential. I turn next to Skinner.

Radical Behaviorism, I: Experimental Foundations

Tolman's chief interest was in cognitive representation. Hull was interested in the process of learning. But both sought the mechanisms that underlie behavior, even if their emphases were different. Hull thought that relatively simple, quantitative principles should suffice to provide a complete explanation. Tolman enjoyed showing that all simple conclusions are false. His best-remembered experiments demonstrate that rats have sophisticated spatial understanding, as opposed to learning through the formation of chains of stimulus-response links. In place of a quantification that he thought premature, Tolman provided metaphorical and impressionistic frameworks out of which he hoped more powerful theories would grow. Neither Hull's simple, if awkwardly expressed, quantitative principles nor Tolman's metaphors have even now led to the comprehensive understanding of behavioral mechanisms that both desired. It was partly impatience with the intractability of the theoretical task that provided the initial impetus to Burrhus Frederick Skinner (1904-1990), the man whose name is now most closely associated with behaviorism.

Skinner's voluminous popular writings made him both the most influential and the most controversial psychologist during the latter part of the twentieth century. His peak of popularity probably exceeded Freud's, at least in the United States. Because so many of his writings are directed at a lay audience, they lack much of the usual scholarly apparatus. His introductory text *Science and human behavior* (1953), for example, cites only a handful of contemporaries, none of them in the psychology of learning, the work's main topic. The book has no references; several of his other influential books have no index, or only a vestigial one. This combination – controversial views, informally presented – is a recipe for misunderstanding, and Skinner's views have often been greatly misrepresented. He was not, for example, a stimulus-response theorist. Nor did he dismiss mental life: he termed mental events 'private events' and treated them like publicly measurable behavior. How successful this was, we will see later. He did not define behavior as 'uninterpreted physical movements' or stimuli as simple physical events. He did not sympathize with or advocate totalitarian regimes (although his persistent use of the word 'control' encourages this interpretation). He did not believe behavior to be exclusively a product of environment, although he used the word frequently and never developed a coherent view of how genetic endowment interacts with environment in the production of behavior.[1]

Skinner's slogan was that behavior should be studied *in its own right* – and not as a mere indicator of unspecified internal mechanisms or processes. He forcefully criticized any explanation of behavior 'which appeals to events taking place somewhere else, at some other level of observation, described in different terms, and measured, if at all, in different dimensions'.[2] In short, he was completely uninterested in behavioral mechanisms of the sort that preoccupied Hull and Tolman. If there are mechanisms, he argued, they are the province of physiology (*neurobiology*, as it would now be termed). Psychology has no need of them. How did Skinner evolve this extreme position? And why was it so influential?

B.F. Skinner began his academic career determined to become a writer.[3] But his early attempts at fiction were unsuccessful and in due course he turned to psychology as a field better suited to his particular mix of talents and his undergraduate preparation in biology. In addition to writing, Skinner was also an ingenious practical mechanic. He liked gadgets and was always inventing new ones. He believed that the history of science shows the value of unplanned, unformalized research: 'If we are interested in perpetuating the practices responsible for the present corpus of scientific knowledge, we must keep in mind that some very important parts of the scientific process do not now lend themselves to mathematical, logical, or any other formal treatment.'[4] In this, of course, he was entirely at odds with the highly formalistic Clark Hull.

Skinner turned this mechanical skill to great practical advantage in his PhD dissertation research, which was on the 'eating reflex' in rats.[5] The research apparently developed in an entirely inductive fashion, guided by a combination of efficiency: 'Some ways of doing research are easier than others' and a lesson from Pavlov: 'Control your conditions and you will see order.' Skinner began by looking at the force exerted by a hungry rat as it ran down a runway to get food. Tired of picking up the rat and placing it at the beginning of the eight-foot runway after each feeding, Skinner added a return path so the rat could return itself. But then he was frustrated by the long waits that developed after each feeding. Once again, the gadget instinct intervened and he modified the square-loop runway so that every circuit by the rat would cause the runway to tilt and operate a primitive automatic feeder. Thus, the rat fed itself by going round the loop. Each rat still sat for a long time at the feeding place before going around again for another run, but Skinner noticed a regularity in the pattern of increasing 'waits' as the animals became satiated. The rotating disk that allowed food pellets to drop had an axle. Seeking better to record the apparently orderly pattern of delays, Skinner attached a cord to the axle. As the cord unwound with each successive feeding, it moved a pen across a steadily turning drum, tracing out the first *cumulative record* of eating behavior (Fig. 2.1). The slope of the curve shows the frequency of eating: as usually drawn the more rapidly the response is repeated, the steeper the slope. Thus, the rats ate rapidly at first, but then the waits became longer, they ate slower and slower as they became satiated. Skinner believed he had found an automatic, behavioral method for measuring the progress of 'hunger.' With the behavior made manifest, the 'internal state' could be dispensed with. Skinner and his collaborators carried this principle forward later, developing experimental procedures to demonstrate a few other internal states like *anxiety* and *fear*. A little later, the Hullian neobehaviorists Dollard and Miller tried to apply behavioristic ideas to clinical and personality issues and later still Hobart Mowrer attempted to capture many other emotional states in behavioral terms.[6] Skinner never mentioned any of this work. He felt no obligation to relate his work to the work of others, and rarely cited his rivals or critics.[7]

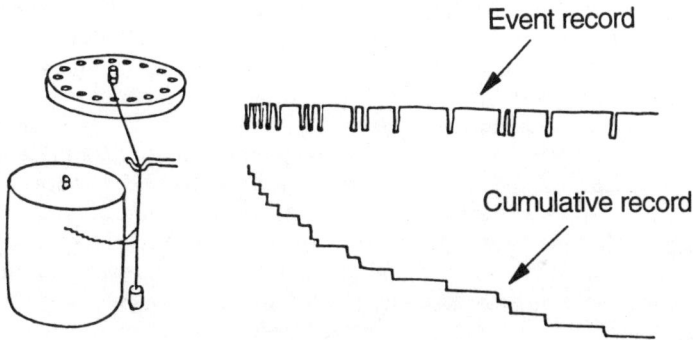

Fig. 2.1. Skinner's first cumulative recorder. With each click of the feeder disk, the recording pen moves downwards. As the drum turns, a cumulative record like the one on the right is produced. The record is upside down because of the mechanical method Skinner used. As usually shown, the record rises as more eating episodes (or operant responses) occur, so that faster the response occurs, the steeper the slope. An event record, showing each response as a 'blip', appears at the top. (From *Cumulative record*, p. 85, by permission.)

Eventually, of course, Skinner saw that the runway was redundant and discarded it. The rat was allowed to produce food by moving a cover over a food tray. In the final adaptation of what had become the *Skinner box*, the rat simply pressed a little metal lever which then operated the feeder electrically. As a result of experience gained during a research project he did for the Department of Defense during the Second World War, Skinner subsequently abandoned rats for pigeons – longer-lived animals, with better vision and more easily controlled by visual stimuli.

Operant behavior. Lever pressing is an example of behavior that Skinner termed *operant behavior*: 'operant' because it operates on the environment, and is *guided by its consequences*. The rat will continue to press so long as food is forthcoming. (Other behaviorists used the term *instrumental* behavior for the same thing, but Skinner always insisted on his own terms.) Operant behavior was said to be *emitted*, in contrast to *respondent* behavior, which was said to be *elicited* by a stimulus. Skinner contrasted 'voluntary' operant behavior with the kind

31

of 'involuntary' respondent behavior, such as salivation, studied by Pavlov and other students of classical, 'Pavlovian' conditioning. The terms 'voluntary' and 'involuntary' are in quotes because it is hard to give exact meaning to the notion of voluntariness when the subject is a rat. The point is that the kinds of activity that are amenable to operant conditioning (i.e. strengthening by consequences) are those that in people are thought of as voluntary: movements of the skeletal musculature. Whereas respondent behavior refers to things like salivation, heart rate or the galvanic skin response which may occasionally be altered by indirect voluntary means (imagining a tragedy to induce crying, for example), but are not ordinarily susceptible to operant reinforcement.

The concept of 'emission' of operant behavior is important. It represents Skinner's recognition that operant behavior must occur spontaneously before it can have consequences or be guided by them. Skinner never inquired into the nature of the process that generates operant behavior in advance of any opportunity for reinforcement. The manufacturers of Rolls-Royce automobiles in their heyday, when asked about the power of their cars, are said to have responded 'sufficient'. Skinner presumably felt this way (he wrote nothing explicit) about the range of spontaneous behavioral variation: variation is sufficient to allow for some act to be reinforced and be strengthened thereby. Skinner's acknowledgment of behavioral spontaneity, no matter how incompletely defined, was nevertheless an important advance in our understanding of the process of instrumental learning.

Reinforcement schedules. Just as Hull's research depended on, and was to some extent conditioned by, statistical techniques, Skinner's to some extent grew out of the cumulative recorder. This method of recording requires a repetitive response, like eating, lever pressing or pecking a disk; it draws attention to the temporal spacing of behavior, represented as a *local rate* – the slope of the record. And a cumulative recorder operates unattended, allowing for very long-term experiments. All these tendencies were further encouraged by Skinner's next discovery, which arose from his first principle: some kinds of research are easier than others. As he tells it, one weekend he ran out of food pellets (which had to be laboriously made by hand at that time). Unwilling to interrupt his research until more could be purchased on Monday, he decided to abandon the standard practice of giving food to the rat for every response. Instead, he delivered a pellet only once a minute, i.e. for the first successful 'response' (cover displacement) a minute or more after the previous one (this would now be termed a *fixed-interval schedule of reinforcement*). Rather to his surprise, his rats continued to respond, and their responding stabilized (apparently) at a steady rate.[8] Response *rate* – number of lever presses or key pecks averaged over times ranging from a few minutes to several hours – was to play a central role in Skinnerian psychology. Skinner believed rate to be a measure of response *probability*, and thought it of fundamental importance – although he never effectively explained why.

In this way, beginning with the study of reflex-like eating behavior, Skinner, his students and collaborators, were led to devote the next few years to the study of *reinforcement schedules*. A massive, untidy compendium of the early work, *Schedules of reinforcement*, written with collaborator Charles Ferster, was published in 1957.[9] In haphazard fashion, it presented hundreds of cumulative records from dozens of pigeons trained often for many hundreds of hours under various schedules (see Figs 2.2 and 2.3). Details of presentation may have seemed unimportant at the time, because of the striking regularities visible in the cumulative-record patterns the pigeons produced under various schedules.

Schedules of reinforcement was organized atheoretically, not in terms of processes, but in terms of *procedures*. Time-based schedules were termed either *fixed* or *variable interval*, according as the time between food opportunities was fixed or determined by some irregular rule. In both fixed- and variable-interval schedules, the time is initiated by a feeding episode (for which the term *positive reinforcement* was now mandated). In *differential-reinforcement-of-low-rate* or *spaced-responding* schedules the timer is reset by each response – so that the animal must wait a fixed number of seconds between each response if he is to get food (most animals find this very difficult). In *ratio* schedules, the first response after a fixed or variable *number* of responses since the previous reinforcement is reinforced. Ratio schedules typically generate high rates of responding (see Figure 2.2).

33

Operant Conditioning Procedures

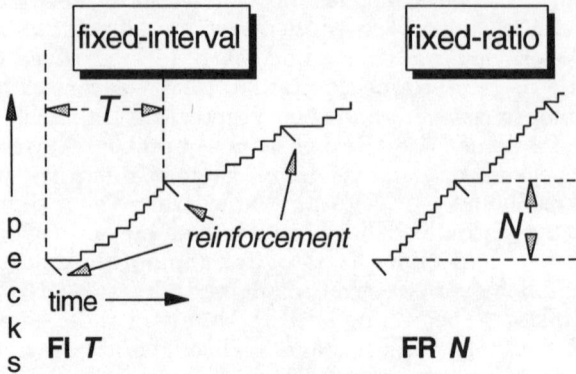

Fig. 2.2. Schematic cumulative records illustrating performance on two common reinforcement schedules: *fixed-interval* and *fixed-ratio*. Pecks cumulate on the vertical axis, time elapses on the horizontal axis. In each case, reinforcement (i.e. food delivery) occurs immediately after the first peck to meet the schedule requirement – either a fixed time (fixed-interval) or a fixed number of pecks (fixed-ratio), since the previous food delivery. Notice that the response rate (slope of the staircase) is higher on the ratio than the interval schedule.

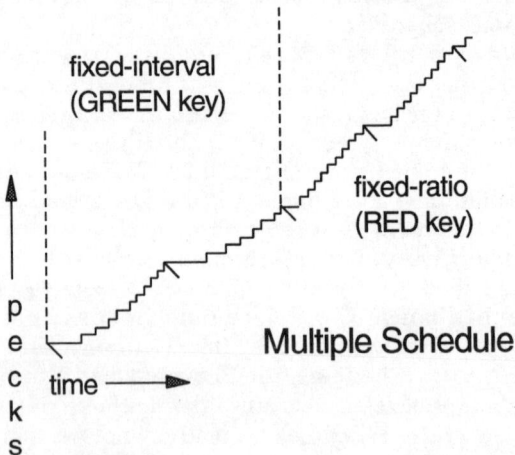

Fig. 2.3. Schematic cumulative record of performance on a multiple fixed-interval, fixed-ratio schedule.

Pigeons soon learn to attend to the color of the transilluminated disk they must peck to get food. Skinner very quickly found that if food is delivered only when the pecking disk (termed a *response key*) is GREEN (say) and not when it is RED, pigeons will soon cease to respond when the RED light comes on. More interestingly, if the schedule of reinforcement when the key is GREEN is different from that when it is RED, pigeons will eventually come to display in the presence of each color the cumulative-record pattern typical of each schedule. This is an example of stimulus *discrimination*, although the technical term *stimulus control* was preferred. The successive-discrimination procedure was termed a *multiple* schedule. Fig. 2.3 shows an example of behavior on a multiple schedule.

Pigeons will learn to peck a key if pecks change the color of the key to a color that has been paired with food. For example, in the presence of a RED key, pecks may be paid off on a fixed-interval schedule by a change in the key color to GREEN. In the presence of GREEN pecks are paid off on a fixed-ratio schedule with food. After food reinforcement, the key changes to RED once again and the cycle is repeated. After experiencing several hundred repetitions of this procedure, usually spread over many days, the pattern of behavior in each of the two *links* will begin to look like the standard pattern for each schedule, obtained after extended training with food reinforcement alone. A procedure like this is termed a *chain* schedule, and the number of 'links' can be extended to five or six, with the final link the only one to end with food, before responding in the early links begins to fall off (i.e. to *extinguish*). Many changes can obviously be rung on the theme of stimuli and reinforcements presented in various sequences and the set has not been exhausted by the legions of *operant conditioners* who learned these methods and explored their implications in the years after the publication of *Schedules of reinforcement*.

It is important not to underestimate the enormous excitement associated with the discovery of reinforcement schedules. After the inevitable estrangement of the experimenter from the individual subject that the older methods entailed, the power of Skinnerian techniques was intoxicating. The visible and orderly output generated moment-by-moment by each subject, the lack of any need for inferential statistics, the amplification of research effort made possible by automation (Skinnerian experiments were soon run automatically by a system of electromagnetic relays, timers and counters), and the new world of possibilities opened up by the reinforcement-schedule idea generated a heady atmosphere among operant conditioners in the 1950s and 1960s. The fact that many different species, from mice through monkeys to men, show essentially the same response patterns on a range of schedules, seemed just to underline the universality of reinforcement schedules as global determiners of behavior.

Murray Sidman in 1960 published an influential methodological book, *The tactics of scientific research*,[10] which provided a systematic rationale for the whole approach. Sidman's inspiring book was a landmark. It provided a reasoned justification for what came to be known as 'within-subject' research (as opposed to the 'between-group' approach of Hull and all other behaviorists) via the notion of behavioral *reversibility*. For example, the distinctive pattern of responding that can be observed on fixed-interval (FI) schedules – a pause in responding after food, followed by responding at an accelerating rate until the next food reinforcement (see Fig. 2.2) – can always be recovered after intervening training on some other procedure. The 'FI scallop' is a *reversible* property of behavior. Once this concept was accepted, it became possible to carry out extensive experiments on reinforcement learning with a handful of subjects. So long as one was careful to restore behavior to the 'baseline' in between experimental conditions, the effect of different independent variables, such as stimuli or other schedules, could be repeatedly measured in the same individual subject. In recent years, the limitations of the reversibility idea have become more apparent.[11] But at the time it was a liberating notion that permitted a vast simplification of research design and a new directness in the experimental analysis of behavior.

As the automation of schedule experiments grew increasingly easy, emphasis shifted from the cumulative record to elapsed-time measures and electromechanical counter totals of responses and reinforcers. There is obviously no limit to the number of different response keys with which a pigeon may be simultaneously confronted. Soon a whole industry arose to study the topic of *choice*, defined as the relative *rates* (number of responses divided by elapsed time) of pecking on two or more simultaneously available response keys, each associated with a different intermittent schedule of reinforcement. (Such arrangements are termed *concurrent* schedules.) In the early 1960s, Skinner's student Richard Herrnstein[12] noticed that under many conditions animals long exposed to a pair of intermittent schedules tend to stabilize at rates of response such that the average payoff probability (total reinforcers divided by total responses, counted over a few hours) is the same for all alternatives, an important relation known as the *matching law*. (Relations between averages like these came to be known as *molar* laws.) Many papers were published on the topic of matching in the years following Herrnstein's 1961 paper.

The *experimental analysis of behavior*, as the Skinnerian movement called itself, grew exponentially during the 1950s and 1960s. Two new journals were founded, the *Journal of the Experimental Analysis of Behavior* (for basic research, largely with animals, in 1958) and *The Journal of Applied Behavior Analysis* (for clinical research, largely with people, in 1968). Skinnerian research became a microcosm of psychology in general, dominated by the ideas of one man. A substantial body of experimental work was produced, but very little theory. The matching-law people were interested in molar *functional relations*, that is steady-state relations between aggregate measures such as response and reinforcement ratios. But, in accordance with Skinner's strictures, there was little interest in 'underlying processes.' The discovery of orderly functional relations was assumed by many Skinnerians (now increasingly calling themselves *behavior analysts*) to exhaust the possibilities of the scientific study of behavior. Powerful experimental methods were developed and many such orderly relations were discovered. This growing body of empirical work was, however, put to polemical use. Skinner's assertions on the general topic of a 'technology of behavior' grew increasingly bold in the 1960s, culminating in his 1971 best-seller *Beyond freedom and dignity*.[13] The experimental research on operant behavior was held up in support of these impressive claims. I will look at the validity of these arguments in the next two chapters.

Behavior analysis international. Skinnerian techniques and ideas were spread all over the world by Skinner's students, postdoctoral associates and the foreign scientists who visited the laboratories at Harvard or Columbia. The Columbia lab was especially important. Fred Keller, a close friend and fellow graduate student with Skinner at Harvard in the early 1930s, went on to Columbia and was a major force in spreading the behavior-analytic word. Keller, a gentle and amiable man and much-beloved teacher, together with a younger somewhat less lovable colleague, William Schoenfeld, wrote the first Skinnerian text in 1950.[14] Keller visited Brazil for a year in 1961 (the first of several such visits), learned Portuguese and helped found the Department of Psychology in Brasilia in 1964. The approach was carried forward by Carolina Bori and (until a military takeover a few years later which devastated the universities and destroyed the lives of many academics) by Rodolfo Azzi.

Brazil might be called the 'Australia of psychology'. Everyone knows the story of how in Australia marsupials, an order little represented elsewhere, have radiated into niches occupied in the rest of the world by placental mammals: a marsupial wolf, a marsupial deer (the kangaroo) a marsupial rat, and so on. Skinnerian psychology in Brazil has radiated into niches occupied elsewhere by other intellectual species. Thus, in Brazil we can find behavior-analytic cognitive psychology, behavior-analytic developmental psychology, behavior-analytic personality psychology, and so on. It is a sociological version of the evolutionists' 'founder effect', the founder in this case being Fred Keller. (Cognitivist critics of Skinner may take comfort in the Australian analogy, feeling that they represent placentals to Skinner's marsupials. They should not celebrate prematurely; the question of extinction is not yet settled!) Skinner and Keller were not the only influences on Brazilian psychology, of course. But the role of radical behaviorism as the founding approach has produced interesting intellectual conjunctions (between Skinnerian and Piagetian approaches, for example) seen nowhere else.

Other early Skinnerian colonies were established in Britain at Birkbeck College in the University of London and Bangor, University College of North Wales, at Liège in Belgium, at Keio University in Japan and, later, at the University of Auckland in New Zealand. Two Mexican behaviorist groups were formed in Mexico City, one in the Harvard tradition (Coyoacan) the other influenced more by Columbia (Iztacala). In recent years, although the number of nonclinical radical behaviorists has probably declined slightly from a peak in the mid-1970s, they are to be found in very many psychology departments, large and small, throughout the world. Radical behaviorist ideas have diffused widely into other areas, particularly psychotherapy and education where Fred Keller's work has been especially important. A very recent development is the incorporation of behavioristic and behavioral-economic ideas into the education of business students in Sardinia.

What has *not* happened (outside Brazil) is any significant fusion of radical behaviorism with other psychological approaches. I will say a few words about why this might be in the final chapter.

Skinnerian explanation

Skinner consistently avoided anything approaching a real theory of learning. Although he always admitted the *possibility* of theory, defined as 'a formal representation of the data reduced to a minimal number of terms',[15] his most frequent comments are highly critical. A historian summarizes his views as follows:

> Skinner admits that 'theories are fun', but he insists that the activity of conjecturing is less efficient than that of observing. Conjecturing appeals to the investigator 'whose curiosity about nature is not equal to his interest in the accuracy of his guesses'. Moreover, conjecturing is said to be 'wasteful', to create 'a false sense of security', and to lead to 'useless' and 'misdirected' experimentation, 'bootless theorizing', and the necessary loss of 'much energy and skill'.[16]

In other places, Skinner acknowledged a place for theory of a limited sort. His book *Contingencies of reinforcement* is subtitled *a theoretical analysis*,[17] but the 'theory' is very far from the kind of formal system favored by other learning theorists and scientists in other areas. Skinner never met a theory he really liked and never developed anything approaching a formal theoretical system. The kind of explanation for behavior favored by Skinnerians is of a very different sort.

Skinner's central explanatory concept is the idea of *reinforcement*, defined more or less as Edward Thorndike defined it in his Law of Effect. Skinner defined reinforcement, as he defined most things, by experimental example. He first describes training a pigeon to stretch its head upwards by reinforcing with food any movement that goes above a line that is continually adjusted upwards (this general technique is known as '*shaping* by successive approximations'). He then goes on to define reinforcement as follows: 'The barest possible statement of the process is this: we make a given consequence contingent [dependent] on certain physical properties of behavior (the upward movement of the head), and the behavior is then observed to increase in frequency.'[18] Any event which will have this frequency-increasing effect if made contingent on behavior – on more than one type of behavior, preferably, so that the definition is not circular – is termed a *reinforcer*. Skinner appropriated the word *contingency* for the dependent, causal, relation between behavior (*response*) and consequence (reinforcer) necessary for the reinforcer to have an effect.

The key term in this definition of reinforcement is *contingency*. It turns out that the way in which behavior determines the occurrence of a reinforcer makes a very great deal of difference to the effectiveness of the reinforcer. The single term *contingency* in fact refers to at least three properties: reinforcement *probability*, *delay* and (in a different, later, sense[19]) *contingency*. The less likely a reinforcer given a response, the weaker its probability-enhancing effect (probability). The longer the time delay between the behavior and the occurrence of the reinforcer, the weaker the effect of the reinforcer (delay). And the more likely a reinforcer is to occur in the absence of the response, the less the effect of those reinforcers that are response-produced (contingency, in the non-Skinnerian sense of a particular kind of predictiveness). The details of these effects are not important. What matters is that the effect of a reinforcer is closely related to what might be termed the *predictiveness* of the response: to the extent that a response is a reliable predictor of a reinforcer, the response will tend to increase in frequency. Thus, the effects of reinforcers are much more complex than the simple, automatic response-strengthening (for Skinner response 'strength' is equivalent to response probability) that Skinner's account implies.

The importance of predictiveness in Pavlovian conditioning was also beginning to be understood in the 1960s: Pavlovian conditioning, like operant conditioning, is facilitated by short delays between conditioned and unconditioned stimuli (the unconditioned stimulus, US, is just a reinforcer in another guise), by high probability of CS-US pairing, and by absence of USs unpaired with the CS.[20] Thus, it was natural for Skinner to combine the two types of relation, Pavlovian (stimulus-reinforcer) and operant (response-reinforcer) into what he called a *three-term contingency* involving stimulus (now termed a *discriminative stimulus*), response and reinforcer. True to form, Skinner never formalized this idea. But it implies an organization of behavior into a collection of more-or-less independent units, by now termed *operants*, each defined by a *classes* of responses and stimuli that jointly predict the occurrence of the relevant reinforcer.[21]

From an experimental point of view, this framework was very fruitful. For example, beginning with a seminal study by George Reynolds in 1961,[22] a whole group of experiments by Reynolds and others began to look at interactions between operants (i.e. violations of the independence assumption). The concept of stimulus control was experimentally refined through various techniques for measuring stimulus *generalization*. Reinforcement schedules are helpful here, because they allow for many unreinforced responses before extinction. A famous experiment by Guttman and Kalish[23] pioneered the technique. Pigeons were trained to peck, on a variable-interval schedule of food reinforcement, a key transilluminated by monochromatic light (at a wavelength of 550 nm, spectral green). Then, food delivery was discontinued and the wavelength was changed randomly every minute. The pigeons nevertheless continued to peck for an hour or more, because of the persistence built in by their training on an intermittent schedule. But the *rate* at which they pecked depended on the wavelength: the farther from 550 nm, the lower the rate. A plot of average rate against wavelength took a peaked form (with the maximum at 550 nm, the training value) that was to become familiar in subsequent years as numerous experiments were carried out with other species and stimulus dimensions. Once again, Skinnerian methods had allowed a hypothetical process – Pavlov's notion of generalization – to be made visible. Thereafter, Skinner was frequently to evoke 'generalization' as an explanation for complex aspects of human behavior, even in situations far removed from wavelength discrimination.

The notion of reinforcement was also expanded, using chain schedules as a model. In a two-link chain schedule, the pigeon pecks a RED key (say) for the reinforcement offered by a change to GREEN, in the presence of which pecks lead to food. The GREEN key was said to be a *conditioned* (or secondary) reinforcer. Although each link in the chain appears to act as a reinforcer for responding that produces it, the whole thing soon collapses if the final food reinforcement is omitted. When there is no food, pigeons soon cease to peck for conditioned reinforcement alone. A stimulus paired with many different reinforcers (food, water, sex) was said to be a *generalized* reinforcer – money was used as a human example. But there are in fact few examples of generalized reinforcers in the animal-research literature.

Operant psychology and economics. Operant behavior is behavior 'guided by its consequences'. Most behavior is guided by its consequences, according to Skinner. Hence, most behavior is operant behavior. The view that most behavior is guided by its effects should be familiar: it is in fact the view of neo-classical *economics*. Economics is the most thoroughgoing application of the idea that behavior adjusts in such a way as to achieve a desired outcome. The differences between economics and Skinnerian behaviorism are differences of emphasis and method. In economics, the usual 'reinforcers' are money and goods. In behavioral psychology they are food (for animals) and money, but also less-well-defined things like 'attention', for people. Economics is more concerned with average behavior of groups of people. As we have seen, Skinner's student Herrnstein and others in the 1960s also became interested in so-called 'molar' behavior, albeit of individuals rather than groups. The behavior-analytic method is primarily experimental; Skinner explicitly avoided formal analysis of reinforcement effects. Most economists are uncomfortable with experiments, but they have developed the formal theory of utility maximization to a high level: Nobelist Herbert Simon has called it '... an impressive body of descriptive ... theory which rivals in mathematical beauty and elegance some of the finest theories in the physical sciences'.[24]

Explaining behavior in terms of reinforcement is very similar to explaining behavior in economic terms. Both methods explain in terms of *outcomes*, reinforcement in the first case, the bundle of goods acquired in the second. There are small differences, however. The neo-classical method in economics is straightforward. The ingredients are the individual's *preference structure* and the set of *constraints* to which he is subject. The preference structure (the well-known *indifference curve* is one way of representing a preference structure) is the set of values (*utilities*) someone attaches to different quantities of the various goods available to him. The set of constraints is the limitations, of budget, time or work schedule, that limit the total quantity of goods he can get. The economist's method is to calculate the allocation of resources (money, time, work, etc.) that will maximize the utility for the subject, given his preference structure and the constraint set.

The reinforcement-theory method is different, although its aim – explaining the subject's allocation of resources (behavior, usually) under a given schedule – is the same. The difference is that reinforcement theory, despite its emphasis on consequences, is not a pure theory of outcomes. As we will see when we get to Skinner's discussion of the 'superstition' experiment, reinforcement is also interpreted mechanistically, as something that strengthens or selects. It has temporal properties: the closer a reinforcer follows a given behavior, the stronger its strengthening effect. This is known as the *delay-of-reinforcement gradient*. Because of its informality (economists would say 'vagueness'), Skinnerian reinforcement theory is much harder to disprove than economic maximization theory.

Reinforcement is usually studied experimentally, and it turns out to be quite easy to devise experimental conditions in which both animal and human subjects behave suboptimally: they fail to act in such a way as to maximize frequency of reinforcement, for example, even though the optimal behavior is apparently well within their capacities (see Box 2.1).[26] Such data pose problems for a simple economic approach. Human beings in the real world doubtless also fail to act optimally, but because realistic experiments (with substantial rewards and punishments, etc.) cannot easily be done, because the real world is complex, and because economists have become extraordinarily ingenious optimality theorists, these failures were largely ignored by economists until quite recently.[27]

Operant psychologists were for years reluctant to see the con-

Box 2.1. Non-optimal behavior in pigeons and people

The diagram below shows a very simple situation in which pigeons fail to show optimal behavior. The diagram shows a single cycle of a procedure called a *response-initiated-delay* (RID) schedule.[25] Sixty or a hundred such cycles constitute a daily experimental session for a hungry pigeon. The cycle begins with brief access to food. Then the pigeon can wait as long or as little as he likes before making his first key peck. The time he waits is labeled t.

```
         wait: t          delay: T
FOOD |_____ | _____ | FOOD

            respond
```

After he responds, a computer-controlled clock starts running and goes for T seconds, at which point food is delivered again. The optimal behavior in this situation is very easy to figure out: the pigeon should respond as soon as he can after food, time t should be set as short as possible – so that the post-peck clock can begin running as soon as possible. Pigeons don't do this. Instead they set time t so that it is a fraction of the *total* interfood interval, $t + T$, that is about the same as if the *whole* time had been fixed at that value by the experimenter. For example, suppose that time T is fixed at 15 seconds; the pigeon's waiting time, t, will be about 5 seconds, the same as if the experimenter had arranged for the total interfood time, $t + T$, to be set at 20 seconds, independently of waiting time. Thus, the pigeon reliably gets food 5 seconds later than necessary.

Lest you think people are significantly smarter, there are situations in human life that work very much along these lines. Who hasn't attended a regular meeting run by a chairman who often comes a little late. The members begin to adjust to the wait by turning up a little late; the chairman, in turn, adjusts to their tardiness by turning up a little later. The meeting begins later and later until someone calls a halt.

vergence between their approach and neo-classical economics, but in the mid-1970s several behavioral psychologists more or less independently noted the resemblances and attempted to explain a number of reinforcement-schedule effects in economic terms. At about the same time, a number of economists began to see that the economic approach might be applied to human psychological topics such as marriage, education, family size, and crime.[28]

*

I have taken some space to describe the details of the operant conditioning method and experimental results, so that when we get to Skinner's extrapolations of these data and methods to human affairs, the nonexpert reader can judge for himself the extent to which they are justified. It should already be obvious that the resemblance between the operant behavior of a pigeon and the operant behavior of a human being is by no means as close as the resemblance between human and animal cells, for example. There are undoubtedly great similarities between pigeons and people. Both will work for reinforcement and when the schedules are the same, the pattern of behavior is also often the same. But the resemblances are at a rather general level. People are sensitive to some schedule properties – sequential, numerical or linguistic properties, for example – that pigeons are not. Food, water and sex are reinforcers for people as well as pigeons, but people are reinforced in many other ways. Often the task for the psychotherapist is to weaken the power of a particular reinforcer (gambling or a narcotic drug, for example), rather than simply apply acceptable reinforcers in more effective ways. Research on reinforcement schedules is much better suited to the latter task than the former. A clever experimenter can easily devise a reinforcement schedule to produce almost any pattern of behavior. But the Skinnerian system is almost silent on what makes a reinforcer reinforcing,[29] and so has nothing to say on why it is, for example, that some people are excessively 'reinforced' by gambling wins whereas others are completely immune to this source of reinforcement, no matter how cleverly scheduled. We will see other difficulties posed by Skinner's extrapolations from pigeons to people in a moment.

3

Radical Behaviorism, II:
Animal Models

For many contemporary researchers the phrase 'animal model' is one word. For most biomedical scientists, animals are of interest only as compliant experimental material whose study may shed light on human problems. The squid has little intrinsic appeal, but attracts experimental attention because its neurons are larger and more accessible than human neurons and seem to function in much the same way. Rat kidney, baboon liver and sea-slug nervous system are all studied for similar reasons. Although Skinner never considered himself a biomedical scientist, his interest in rats and pigeons was strictly of the animal-model variety. He was unimpressed by the growing body of work pioneered by zoologists W.H. Thorpe, Konrad Lorenz, Niko Tinbergen, Karl von Frish and their students on the instinctive and natural behavior of animals. The rich findings of *ethology*, as the zoological approach to animal behavior came to be called in the 1950s, were of little interest to Skinner. In the empiricist (*contra* nativist) behaviorist tradition, he paid only lip service to those genetic and evolutionary factors that differentiate one individual or animal species from another. This neglect was to cause problems for the Skinnerian approach in the late 1960s.

Despite the lack of detailed correspondence between pigeons and people, and even between the experimental situations in which pigeons are studied and those in which people naturally find themselves, the animal-model idea worked powerfully for Skinner. He was as uninterested in detailed correspondences as his popular audience was unaware of experimental minutiae. It was a match made in heaven. To illustrate, I will describe one of Skinner's most compelling extrapolations from the experimental laboratory to human affairs, the so-called 'superstition' experiment. In the course of this account, we will also see how the first experimental cracks began to appear in the Skinnerian system.

The 'superstition' experiment

In his middle and later years, Skinner himself did surprisingly little experimental work to test or even to exploit his ideas. His students and disciples at Harvard, Columbia, Walter Reed and a few other places did many experiments using the operant-conditioning method and explored the world of reinforcement schedules. Almost none of these experiments were direct tests of Skinner's theoretical position, however. (Skinner's proscription of the hypothetico-deductive approach worked very much in his favor here.) Increasingly, Skinner's own gaze was directed elsewhere, to human behavior, which was always his chief interest. He used experimental results only as models for his analysis of human problems. Skinner's 1948 paper ' "Superstition" in the pigeon'[1] is one of the earliest and most dramatic examples of this strategy.

The experiment was incredibly simple. Skinner took a hungry pigeon that had learned to eat from an automatic feeder, but had received no other training. The pigeon was placed in a Skinner box and given brief access to food every 12 seconds (this is the procedure Pavlov called 'temporal conditioning' – see Fig. 1.1). The result was that after a few dozen feedings, every pigeon Skinner tried began to show vigorous, stereotyped activity. This result is surprising, because the birds had no control over food delivery: all they were required to do was wait, and eat when food became available every few seconds. The birds' vigorous activity was completely unnecessary.

This paper shows Skinner's flexibility as an experimenter; it shows his rhetorical genius; and it shows how he could vault effortlessly from a laboratory curiosity to the most exalted aspects of human culture.

Experimental flexibility. The experiment is unique in Skinner's *oeuvre* because it presents observational, rather than automatically gathered, data: nearly all subsequent experimental papers by Skinner and other operant conditioners eschewed all but counter readings and cumulative records. Observational

47

data were generally regarded as unacceptable. Yet the master, more adaptable than his followers, presented simple, anecdotal observations without apology. To study such a procedure, using such a method of gathering data, was a creative departure for someone whose whole career until that time had been devoted to instrumental learning.

Rhetorical genius. Skinner's rhetoric was brilliant, because the results of the experiment – vigorous activity, despite lack of any operant response requirement – would by most neutral observers surely have been interpreted as contrary to his ideas about the indispensability of 'consequences' as a molder of behavior. The pigeons' behavior had *no* consequences. So why did it occur? The 'conditioning' of vigorous skeletal activities by response-independent food delivery might well have been taken then (as they were later) as strong evidence *against* Skinner's view that *contingency* (his view for *dependency* or *causal linkage*) between response and reinforcer is essential to operant conditioning. The obvious interpretation is one that draws on the principles not of operant but of *Pavlovian* conditioning. How did Skinner combat what must surely have occurred to him as an alternative account for his results?

He attacked the problem frontally, in the first paragraph of the paper, by predicting the outcome of the experiment as a deduction from operant reinforcement theory. Presenting new data (whether anticipated or not) as a logical deduction from existing theory has long been a convention in many areas of science. My own guess is that Skinner's choice of this method of presentation was a rhetorical device rather than an accurate account of how he actually came to do the experiment, because he elsewhere argued repeatedly against the hypothetico-deductive approach and, as far as I know, followed it in no other paper. It is hard to believe, therefore, that Skinner's use of the method here was for anything but purposes of persuasion. I doubt that the hypothesis preceded the experiment. Skinner begins the paper as follows:

> To say that a reinforcement is contingent upon a response may mean nothing more than that it follows the response. It may follow because of some mechanical connection [contingency] or because of the mediation of another organism; but conditioning takes place presumably because of the

temporal relation only, expressed in terms of the order and proximity of response and reinforcement. Whenever we present a state of affairs which is known to be reinforcing at a given level of [food] deprivation, we must suppose that conditioning takes place even though we have paid no attention to the behavior of the organism in making the presentation. A simple experiment demonstrates this to be the case.

The ingenuity of this first paragraph is remarkable. The 'mays' and 'must supposes' tend to expel from the reader's mind all sorts of inconvenient counter examples. In hindsight, these hidden questions pop into the foreground: To say that a reinforcement is contingent on a response does *not* mean only that it follows the response (*contiguity*). It also means at least two other things: that reinforcement cannot occur (or occurs less often) in the absence of the response and that reinforcement occurs more often if the response occurs more often. Skinner's rhetoric had the effect of focusing people's attention on contiguity to the exclusion of the other properties of contingency. Persuading his audience in this way was no mean feat, because in all practical matters contingency (the response is necessary for the reinforcer) – which implies all three properties – is the view that prevails. In clinical behavior modification, for example, an undesirable behavior is abolished by omitting reinforcers normally contingent on it, or by delivering contingent punishment; a desirable behavior is strengthened by making reward contingent on it.

Response contingency in Skinner's sense is a procedural feature, not a behavioral process – contingencies must act through some proximal mechanism. Skinner's setup for the superstition paper was aided by the fact that the mechanism for reinforcement was then widely thought to be nothing more than response-reinforcer contiguity. The contiguity view also prevailed about the learning of CS-US relations in classical conditioning. At the time of Skinner's original superstition experiment, the empirical inadequacy of simple contiguity theory to account for either classical or operant conditioning was not well understood.

Skinner explained the vigorous, stereotyped behavior of his pigeons in between periodic food deliveries by means of what he called *adventitious reinforcement,* that is, accidental contiguity between food and a behavior that originally occurs for 'other reasons'. His argument begins with the assumption that a hungry pigeon is not passive in a situation where it receives occasional food. Suppose it happens to be doing something towards the end of an interfood interval and food is delivered. The behavior will be contiguous with the food and so, by the reinforcement principle, will be more likely to occur again. If the next food delivery comes quite soon, this same behavior might still be occurring, and so receive another accidental pairing with food, be further strengthened, occur again in the next interval, and so on. By means of this positive-feedback process, some behavior might be raised to a very high probability.

Since there is no real causal relation between behavior and reinforcer, Skinner called the behavior 'superstitious', by analogy with human superstitions – which he believed to arise in a similar way.

This plausible account was not based on direct observation of the process he described. No one had actually recorded these accidental response-reinforcer contiguities or the progressive increase in response strength that was supposed to follow them. Indeed, the contiguity view, in this impressionistic form, is almost immune to disproof. For example, even in 1948 there was some understanding that the delivery of 'free' reinforcers on a response-contingent schedule might tend to weaken the instrumental (i.e. reinforced) response (this was demonstrated experimentally several years later). This weakening was explained by the hypothesis that if, for some unexamined reason, a behavior other than the instrumental response should happen to occur, then by chance it would sometimes be contiguous with the occasional free reinforcers. This would tend to strengthen 'other' behavior and thus, by competition, weaken the reinforced response. No careful observations were done to substantiate this hypothesis: Did such behaviors occur? How often were they contiguous with free food? What is the form of behavioral competition? Did the frequency of the instrumental response drop before or after such accidental pairings? No quantitative details were given: How many accidental pairings are needed to produce how much increment in strength? How often should unreinforced 'other' behaviors be expected to occur? Thus the view was difficult to refute.

The simple contiguity account of reinforcement poses a difficult methodological problem. It is a causal hypothesis where the cause, response-reinforcer contiguity, *is not under experimental control*: the experimenter can control the contiguity aspect, but the *animal* determines when it will make the response. Inability to control the occurrence of the response makes it impossible to be sure of the effect of any particular pairing between response and reinforcer. For example, suppose the response occurs and we at once deliver a reinforcer, thus ensuring response-reinforcer contiguity. Suppose that a few additional responses then occur; have we demonstrated a strengthening effect of contiguity? Not at all; perhaps this response just happens to occur in runs, so that one response is usually followed by others, quite apart from any reinforcing effect. This is not uncommon — a pigeon will rarely make just one peck, for example. Suppose we reinforce a second response, just to be sure. After a few repeats, no doubt the pigeon is pecking away at a good rate; have we then demonstrated an effect? Again, not really. By repeating the pairings of response and reinforcer we have now established a real *dependency* between response and reinforcer. Perhaps the increase in pecking is just the result of some other process that allows the pigeon to detect such *molar contingencies*, as they are called.

The point, of course, is that in the absence of any proposal for a specific real-time *mechanism* for the action of reinforcement, the hypothesis of adventitious reinforcement is almost unverifiable. Unless behavior in the absence of reinforcement is highly predictable, unless a single reinforcement reliably produces an immediate enhancing effect, preferably on more than one response type, the meaning of those occasional instances where responding seems to increase rapidly following a single contiguous reinforcer is conjectural. A few apparently confirming observations have appeared.[2] But there have been no convincing experimental proofs of the adventitious-reinforcement hypothesis as a process with anything like the generality often assumed for it.

Grand extrapolation. No doubt the very obscurity of these theoretical points, together with the simplicity of the experimental method, combined to add plausibility to Skinner's account of 'superstition'. But the main reason for the success of this paper, and of Skinner's other writings, lies elsewhere: in his ready extension of dry data from the animal operant laboratory to provocative aspects of human social existence – like *superstition*. The leap here is quite substantial, from pigeons posturing in a box to rituals in card games and body language by bowlers and, in Skinner's later writings, to religious beliefs. It rests not so much on any convincing isomorphism between the pigeon in the box and the human situation – where is temporal contiguity and frequent reinforcement in a card game, for example? – as on the reader's empathy with the pigeon. 'The bird behaves as if there were a causal relation ...'[3] writes Skinner, and the reader nods assent.

Many possibilities are suggested by the two words 'as if'! Is reinforcement the source of all knowledge? Is human knowledge as illusory as the pigeon's mistaken causal inference in the superstition experiment? Christians behave 'as if' there were a God, scientists 'as if' truth exists, and all of us 'as if' the floor will not open up under our feet. Are all these 'superstitions'? Are all to be explained by reinforcement? As we shall see in the next chapter, Skinner would probably have answered 'Yes'.

Experimental problems with Skinner's account

Skinner's account of laboratory 'superstition' stood unchallenged for twenty years. The first cracks appeared in 1968 with the publication of a paper by Brown and Jenkins on what they called *autoshaping*. A subsequent paper by Williams and Williams,[4] using the same procedure, established that operant key pecking could be produced and maintained by purely Pavlovian procedures. In these experiments, pigeons untrained to peck a response key are simply allowed to experience occasional pairing of a seven-second key illumination with (at the end) access to food. The procedure reliably produces key pecking after a couple of dozen pairings – even if key pecks have no effect at all. (Or even if pecks actually prevent food.)

A couple of years before Brown and Jenkins published their arresting results, Virginia Simmelhag and I had repeated Skinner's 1948 experiment, and observed the pigeons' behavior second-by-second in the brief interval between feedings from the very beginning of training. We found three things that differ from Skinner's account: (a) The activities that develop are of two kinds: variable *interim activities*, which occur in the first two-thirds or so of the interfood interval and are rarely contiguous with food, and a single *terminal response*, which occurs during the last third. (b) The terminal response is either pecking or a stereotyped pacing activity obviously related to it; the topography (form) of the terminal response does not differ from animal to animal in the irregular way Skinner described. (c) Terminal pecking does not develop in the accidental way implied by the adventitious reinforcement hypothesis. These findings have been repeated many times by others and the details are now quite familiar. We now know that the empirical realities of superstitious behavior are not as tidy as Skinner's account suggests – and we understand better the gaps in his theoretical account. In a lengthy experimental and theoretical paper in 1971[5] we described these results and, drawing on our results and the autoshaping data just described, proposed an alternative account.

Skinner's theory is deficient in two main respects: First, he minimized the importance of the processes that originate novel (i.e. previously unreinforced) behavior – Simmelhag and I termed these processes behavioral *variation*. Skinner's exclusive emphasis was on reinforcement as an agent for response *selection* (more on Skinner's Darwinian approach to reinforcement in a moment). Secondly, he, and most other behaviorists at the time, accepted contiguity as a sufficient process for response selection. Rescorla and Wagner (see Chapter 1) showed later for classical conditioning that *competition* is an essential complement to contiguity: only the two together can provide a mechanism for the detection of contingency (predictability). It is the competition for a finite quantity of 'associative value' that endows the influential Rescorla-Wagner model with its predictive power. Recently, Ying Zhang and I[6] have made a similar formal argument for operant conditioning: contiguity plus competition among action tendencies is sufficient for an *assignment-of-credit* mechanism that can detect true instrumental contingency between response and reinforcer. This mechanism shows for the first time the limitations on Skinner's adventitious reinforcement idea – which can work as Skinner suggested, but only under unrealistic circumstances – and provides a mechanistic account for 'instinctive drift' and other 'misbehaviors' of organisms.[7]

The 'competition' idea is not new, but its relation to contiguity and reinforcement was not at first understood. The idea is very simple. Let us suppose, with Thorndike, Skinner, and most other behaviorists, that if food follows immediately on some response, the response will increase in probability (this idea is much simpler than the truth, but it will do to illustrate my point). When the response occurs, and no food follows, response probability will decrease. If a response is reinforced only intermittently, then it will occur at some intermediate rate, representing a balance between the strengthening effects of the occasional food delivery, and the weakening effects of occurrences not followed by food. Now suppose we give a few 'free' food deliveries. Very few of these will be contiguous with the 'reinforced' response, but they may be contiguous with something else the animal happens to be doing when it isn't making the 'reinforced' response. Now, *if* these 'other' activities are significantly strengthened, and *if* they interfere (i.e. compete) with the 'reinforced' response, then by *adding* 'free' reinforcement we may actually weaken the 'reinforced' response. This weakening is the effect of contingency (in its second sense) that I described in Chapter 2. The process that Zhang and I proposed in 1991 is a formal demonstration that competition can have the effects I have described.

So response *selection* seems to involve (at least) both contiguity and competition. As for behavioral *variation*, the autoshaping work showed that stimulus-reinforcer (CS-US) pairing is sufficient to generate pecking 'conditioned' to the CS. Simmelhag and I extended the argument to suggest that Pavlovian procedures always generate a *repertoire* of activities conditioned to the CS. It just so happens that when the subject is a hungry pigeon, the stimulus is highly predictive, and the reinforcer is food, that repertoire is dominated by pecking. 'Classical conditioning', in short, functions in operant conditioning as one of the major mechanisms of behavioral variation.

If skeletal, 'operant' responses can be produced through classical conditioning procedures – as autoshaping and the superstition experiment both show – then Skinner's distinction between operant behavior (conditionable only by consequential reinforcement) and respondent behavior (conditionable only by Pavlovian means) ceases to be useful. Salivation, the prototypical Pavlovian response, is of course physiologically different from pecking and lever pressing (the prototypical operant responses). Salivation, a *respondent*, in Skinner's terms, is controlled by the autonomic nervous system, lever pressing, an operant response, by the skeletal system. The point is that the terms 'operant' and 'respondent' add nothing to these physiological differences if the terms fail to correspond to sharp differences in susceptibility to operant and Pavlovian conditioning. Pecking, and a number of other activities in other species, has both operant and respondent properties. Thus, the operant-respondent distinction no longer seemed as useful as before.

What of Skinner's 'as if' account? In what sense do superstitious pigeons behave 'as if' their responses produce food? Well, not in the sense that they cannot tell the difference. Peter Killeen[8] showed convincingly that when pigeons must respond differentially depending on whether a particular food delivery is produced by their own pecking, or by a computer that mimics their pecking, they do very well indeed. Pigeons can detect extraordinarily small differences in temporal contiguity – much smaller than those they experience under the fixed-time 'superstition' schedule. If they continue to peck when pecking is irrelevant it is certainly not because they are unable to discriminate pecks that produce food from pecks that don't.

Despite argument and experiment, the 'as if' account shows signs of outliving every other idea in the 'superstition' paper. The idea has important philosophical implications. Perhaps we do nothing from real *knowledge*; indeed the idea of knowledge is itself suspect. We do everything only because of things that have happened to us in the past, our *reinforcement history*. To the minor objection that reflexes, digestion and so forth are activities not easily traced to reinforcement history, Skinner has responded with an evolutionary argument: if not your history, then the history of your ancestors. His epistemology, as befits an intellectual descendant of William James, is just the ultimate form of *pragmatism*: 'truth' is what produces reinforcement.

These ideas have taken root in some strange lands, most recently in the politically-correct thickets of literary theory. The dissolution of knowledge seems to be especially attractive to the more advanced humanistic scholars. Indeed, many find the idea liberating. It certainly elevates literary theory and devalues natural science. In these weedy literary groves, knowledge is replaced by opaque pseudo-philosophies that look to outsiders like parodies of all the worst features of hyperspecialized and fractionated modern social science. Readers willing to brave the hermetic prose of critical theory will find here and there descendants of Skinner's pragmatic linguistic philosophy.[9] In his later years, Skinner was to embrace a pragmatic, evolutionary epistemology explicitly. I take up this theme in the next chapter.

The Darwinian metaphor

Beginning in the mid-1960s, Skinner modified his approach to learned behavior. In a paper entitled 'The phylogeny and ontogeny of behavior'[10] he turned to a view of reinforcement quite different from the 'strengthening' metaphor he had adopted earlier. Instead of strengthening, reinforcement was now said to 'select' behavior, much as natural selection acts to favor certain individuals for survival and reproduction. And just as adaptation in nature can be traced to selection, so adaptation to contingencies of reinforcement was said to reflect the selective action of reinforcement.

The identification of reinforcement ('reward' in an older language) as an agent of selection was not a new idea. The psychologist James Baldwin had advanced it early in the twentieth century, Clark Hull at least mentioned it between the wars[11] and W.R. Ashby, D.T. Campbell and philosopher Karl Popper had elaborated on the idea in different ways in the post-war years.[12] No doubt Darwin somewhere in his many works speculates along similar lines. Skinner made little use of the idea as an explanation for reinforcement-schedule effects. Its chief role there was to provide a rather 'pat' account for reinforcement itself ('reinforcement' being the unmoved mover in his previous account). Reinforcers are reinforcing, said Skinner, because animals reinforced by appropriate food (say) are favored in phylogeny (i.e. in the evolution of the species). Thus, 'what is reinforcing' is determined by what Skinner termed 'phylogenic' contingencies (once again, Skinner insisted on his own word: 'phylogenetic' would be the consensual term). 'What is done' (i.e. operant behavior) is then determined by 'ontogenic' contingencies – contingencies of reinforcement.

The account led to the usual ingenious extrapolations. Thus, obesity in the modern world is explicable, said Skinner, by the fact that high-calorie substances containing sugar taste sweet and are much preferred over low-calorie foods. In our 'selection environment' in the remote past these beneficial substances (as well as fats and proteins) were rare. Thus, individuals strongly reinforced by sweetness, hence motivated to seek out sweet things, were favored in the race to reproduce. But because sugar was rare, there was no negative selection for over-indulgence. Today in the developed world sweet things are widely available, are eaten to excess by many people and cause unhealthy obesity. We are victims, says Skinner, of changes in our environment; changes too rapid for natural, phylogenic, selection to keep up with. This is as plausible as most evolutionary 'Just-So' stories,[13] but it added nothing to what was already known, and is little help in understanding the details of learning in animals.

Some efforts were made by other behaviorists to apply the evolutionary metaphor to the specifics of learning. One of the earliest was a lengthy discussion of the relations between selection and behavioral variation by Simmelhag and myself. The key point in our account is that processes of behavioral *variation* are just as important as processes of *selection*. Variation and selection were of equal importance to Darwin and his successors; they must be of equal importance in the application of the Darwinian idea to operant behavior. Variation, the processes that generate behavior in advance of operant reinforcement, is often much more important than selection. In teaching difficult concepts (in mathematics, for example), the hard task for the teacher is to get the child to 'understand' the concept for the very first time, not to 'increase the frequency' of some simple behavior. It is getting the 'behavior' for the very first time that is critical, not its subsequent maintenance. This problem cannot even be attacked, much less solved, without some grasp of mechanisms of variation.

Skinner made no attempt to specify the mechanisms of variation. Indeed, in his famous simile, 'Operant conditioning shapes behavior as a sculptor shapes a lump of clay',[14] he implies, as we put it, that 'moment-to-moment variation is small in magnitude, and essentially random ... in direction'.[15] Like Darwin, Skinner was a gradualist. But unlike Darwin, who was well aware of the existence of large and often directional phenotypic changes from generation to generation, Skinner never seriously considered the possibility that variation might be structured or constrained. But in fact, if operant conditioning is a sculptor, it is a sculptor in wood, with its grain and knots, rather than a sculptor in isotropic clay.

We pointed out that even in Darwin's time, when the beautiful mechanisms of molecular genetics were unknown, he was nevertheless able to identify several factors that affect variation in phylogenetic evolution. Darwin noted that a change in conditions, or relaxation of selection, can both cause great increases in the range of variation, and there is little reason to doubt that similar effects can occur in ontogeny under the action of reinforcement. In experimental extinction (cessation of reinforcement), for example, the range of variation typically increases at first.

Stimulus context constrains, sustains and directs behavioral variation. For example, Pavlovian conditioning, which allows a particular neutral stimulus to acquire signal properties, will itself give rise to a repertoire of reinforcer-related activities from which operant reinforcement can then select. A stimulus associated with food, or even food itself in a novel context, will induce a wide range of food-related activities from which operant reinforcement (if such is available) can then select. But if the range of induced activities is limited, then the power of operant reinforcement to mold behavior will also be limited, in ways that may conflict with standard reinforcement accounts. The autoshaping procedure discussed earlier is an example. Given a highly predictive stimulus, then pecking (in pigeons) may be the *only* activity induced, so that a contingency involving some other activity can have no effect.

Selection can of course affect variation, and this process is also well known in biological evolution. In *frequency-dependent selection*, for example, rare types are especially favored. Frequency-dependent selection can give rise to a population that is highly variable in form, because each new variant has an advantage. Reinforcement schedules with the property of frequency dependence have been shown to give rise to highly variable behavior, presumably for the same reason.[16]

Quite surprising details of reinforcement effects parallel selective effects in phylogeny. For example, there is a phenomenon of instinctive behavior known as *supernormal stimuli*. A supernormal stimulus is a stimulus never seen under natural conditions that is nevertheless more effective than the natural

Fig. 3.1. An oystercatcher retrieving an artificial, super-large egg in preference to its own, smaller egg.

stimulus. Fig. 3.1 shows an example: in preference to its own egg, an oystercatcher is retrieving a much larger artificial egg. There is a comparable phenomenon in discrimination learning. An animal trained to respond to one stimulus (say a wavelength of 550 nm) which is alternated with another (at 500 nm) in the presence of which it never gets any food, in a test may well show maximal responding at 600 nm, i.e. at a point on the wavelength dimension displaced away from the negative (500 nm) stimulus. Perhaps these phenomena both reflect *asymmetrical* selection.[17] In the operant case, the subject is trained to respond at 550 and to suppress responding to 500. It never sees 600 in training, so there is no selection against responding to 600, which is why it is favored over 550 in a generalization test. In the phylogenetic case, the normal egg is favored, but retrieval of smaller-than-normal eggs may be selected against because they are likely to be unviable. Larger-than-normal eggs are never encountered in nature (for mechanical reasons, presumably); hence they may be favored when encountered under artificial conditions.

The Darwinian metaphor allows Skinnerian behaviorism to explain behavior in terms of consequences without falling into the trap of economic rationalism.[18] If consequences are all that matter, then all consequences must be known. The *rational man* will then act so as to bring about the most desirable consequence. Perfect rationality thus presupposes omniscience. If all consequences cannot be known, then some principled limitations on knowledge must be discovered – this is known as *bounded rationality*. These cognitive limitations in effect constitute a causal psychology which, if known in full, renders the search for consequences unnecessary. This argument raises doubts about the ultimate value of a psychology based entirely on consequences.

A psychology based on the Darwinian metaphor does not fall into this trap, because consequences can select only from the options offered up by variation. The options are selected according to the principles of reinforcement; and the set of options is determined by mechanisms of behavioral variation. Both variation and selection limit the range of possible actions that need be considered, so that omniscience is not necessary, behavior need not be 'optimal' in any sense, and rationality forms no part of the account.

Intrinsic to the Darwinian metaphor is the distinction between *phenotype* and *genotype*. The phenotype is the visible outcome of the developmental process, the whole organism with its morphology and behavior. The phenotype is what makes contact with the environment and is subject to the 'contingencies of survival'.[19] But it is the genotype that is inherited, so that only those phenotypic characteristics that have a genetic counterpart can take part in the evolutionary process. The generations of spaniel pups that have had their tails docked at birth have not given rise to a race of tailless spaniels.

The phenotype-genotype distinction is uncomfortably similar to the neo-behaviorist distinction between performance and learning, which Skinner had always rejected. He was consistent in never admitting that the phenotype-genotype distinction might also apply to operant behavior, even though it is part and parcel of the Darwinian metaphor. The distinction nevertheless reflects well-known facts. Only some things that animals do can be selected through operant reinforcement. Distinguishing those that can from those that cannot requires an understanding of the relations between the internal processes that generate overt actions and the actions themselves – the behavioral equivalent of the laws of development that translate genotype into phenotype. It also requires an understanding of the differences between those internal states that have successors across time, i.e. *memories*, and those internal states that leave no imprint on the future. Since Skinner never accepted the idea of internal states, which are implied by the genotype-phenotype distinction, he failed to apply the Darwinian metaphor in a thoroughgoing way.

In his 1966 paper Skinner seemed concerned to show evolutionists what they could learn from operant conditioning. He was much less attentive to what he might learn from the evolutionists, hence missed many opportunities to test Darwinian ideas in operant conditioning experiments.

A serious problem with the Darwinian metaphor is that it can be applied in so many different ways – and there is often no easy way to distinguish empirically among them. What we can say is that Skinner's application was neither original nor profound. Even in the area of human social arrangements, always Skinner's main focus, much better attempts have been made. D.T. Campbell, for example, in a modestly presented and carefully reasoned account, identified sources of conflict between 'selfish' propensities favored by individual genetic selection, and 'altruistic' propensities favored by cultural evolution within groups. Campbell's claims were cautious: 'You are hereby warned – this talk is not hardheaded science but an exercise in quasi-scientific speculation.'[20] He frequently reminds his readers that real-life social questions cannot be the subject of meaningful experiments, and that our ignorance of fundamentals severely limits our ability to generalize from laboratory situations to the world at large. Campbell's heavily documented, highly qualified account is much harder going than Skinner's confident, deceptively simple presentation of the Darwinian metaphor. But truth-in-advertising would have required Skinner to begin with Campbell's warning – in boldface.

In recent years, a new field of *evolutionary psychology* has come into being which seeks to apply the Darwinian metaphor in systematic and testable ways to human behavior.[21] This work has developed in the careful tradition of Campbell, not on the go-for-broke lines of radical behaviorism.

*

Skinner's interest in research with animals was purely analogical. He had little interest in phylogeny and species-specific behavior, the topics studied by ethologists like Lorenz and Tinbergen. For Skinner, as for the biomedical community, animals are simply convenient preparations with which to demonstrate effects that have human analogues. His approach was to take experimental results (rather than theoretical principles) from the animal laboratory and extrapolate them persuasively to human behavior. I illustrated this approach with a discussion of the so-called 'superstition' experiment, a simple procedure which generates vigorous but unnecessary activity in pigeons and in many other animal species. By presenting this result as a prediction of the informal contiguity theory of reinforcement, and by invoking the reader's empathy with the pigeon in his 'as-if' account, Skinner was able to convince his audience that many human superstitions – and many puzzling effects in the operant laboratory – simply reflect the ubiquitous effects of operant reinforcement. The superstition experiment is interesting for two reasons. First, because it illustrates the subtleties of Skinner's rhetorical method, and second because it was a focus for a series of experiments and theoretical developments that eroded the early simplicities of Skinnerian reinforcement theory.

The response of Skinner and others to these developments was increased emphasis on the *Darwinian metaphor*, the analogy between reinforcement and natural (or artificial) selection. Skinner emphasized the selection aspect – reinforcement '... shapes behavior as a sculptor shapes a lump of clay ...'. But others were more even-handed and placed equal emphasis on the selective action of reinforcement and the limiting role of behavioral *variation* in providing material on which reinforcement can act. For reasons to do with his consistent emphasis on ways to *change* behavior, Skinner was apparently reluctant to take the problems of variation seriously. Consequently, he applied the Darwinian metaphor in a half-hearted and ultimately ineffective way.

4

Radical Behaviorism and Society

'Behaviorism is not the science of human behavior; it is the philosophy of that science.'[1] writes Skinner in *About behaviorism*, the popular successor to *Beyond freedom and dignity*.[2] The Darwinian metaphor, which Skinner applied only half-heartedly to the details of operant conditioning in animals, was put to philosophical use in his evolutionary epistemology. This approach to knowledge is fundamental to Skinner's societal prescriptions. Since Skinner's fame with the public at large rests almost exclusively on his extrapolations from laboratory to society, some examination of his epistemology is in order.

This task is not as simple as it might seem, because Skinner's writings slip seamlessly between science (the facts and methods of operant conditioning) and radical behaviorism, the underlying philosophy of science.[3] Nevertheless, we can identify two key themes: knowledge and value as the products of evolution, and the radical behaviorist view of mental life. Let's look first at the larger theme.

Truth, justice, value and natural selection

Evolutionary epistemology (EE: see earlier references to Popper and Campbell) is the notion that knowledge is a product of our evolutionary history.[4] Nothing is certain – not logic, not the hand in front of your face, not the child you see through the window. Everything we appear to know (says EE) is the outcome of millions of years of natural selection – and thousands of years of cultural selection. Thus, our belief in logic is firm not because logic is 'true' in some eternal, Platonic sense, but because those individuals and cultures that failed to believe in logic lost out in the struggle to reproduce. We believe in tables and chairs, in other people, and in their minds, not because these things are true either, but because such beliefs were effective in the battle of life. A consistent evolutionary epistemologist would go on (as D.T. Campbell did) to contend that our value systems and religious beliefs have also survived a rigorous history and on that account have some degree of 'truth'.

Truth. Evolutionary epistemology denies the existence of absolute truth – although the existence of some more or less stable 'external reality' within which natural selection can take place is tacitly assumed. Denial of truth is rightly disturbing to many people, not least because '… the idea that there is no such thing as objective truth … [is] closely linked with authoritarian and totalitarian ideas'.[5] Nevertheless, some thinkers have proposed abandonment of the idea of truth. In its place they propose locutions such as 'relatively permanent beliefs' or 'consensually agreed beliefs'. These substitutes are unsatisfactory – and unnecessary. Evolutionary epistemology in fact entails no real change in what scientists do, or even in what they believe, despite the assertions of relativists. The key point about evolutionary epistemology is just that the 'truth' of any proposition *is relative to the challenges it has successfully met*. Thus, a belief that has been unquestioned for a thousand years is likely to be less 'true' than one that has emerged unscathed from numerous tests (although the test of time is certainly worth something, as I will argue in a moment). The fact that people agree on something is also irrelevant, if they have never questioned it. Permanence and consensus are only indirectly related to truth, as EE views it.

There are a few beliefs, like the laws of logic or arithmetic, the belief that the chair I am sitting in is real, and so on, that have survived every conceivable test. Such beliefs are the best kind of truth we have. When we ask of some new proposition 'Is it true?' all we mean (says EE) is 'Will it be as resistant to disproof as the laws of logic?' In effect, those beliefs that are most resistant to disproof become the standard by which the truth of others is judged. Since this is how scientists are supposed to judge truth anyway, evolutionary epistemology poses no practical threat to the traditional belief in the possibility of truth. This will be disappointing to totalitarians, and some literary theorists, but it will be reassuring to others.

Skinner's epistemology. Like his application of the Darwinian metaphor to operant behavior, Skinner's evolutionary epistemology is both extreme and inconsistent. He elevates behavioristic analysis above everything else, logic included. In an early discussion of the philosophical basis for behaviorism, for example, he writes: 'If it turns out that our final [EE] view of verbal behavior invalidates our scientific structure from the point of view of logic and truth-value, then so much the worse for logic, which will also have been embraced by our analysis.'[6] On the other hand, unlike Campbell, he gives traditional beliefs little credit, despite the fact that they are as much products of our evolution as anything else. All in all, Skinner found orthodox moral values and beliefs about human nature to be less useful evolutionary products than radical behaviorism. Indeed, in his later writings he systematically undermined traditional beliefs, substituting values supposedly derived from evolutionary considerations. What was the purpose of these attacks, and how successful are they?

Skinner's critique of responsibility

Skinner's method can be inferred from two passages in *Beyond freedom and dignity*.[7] The book is concerned with the application of a 'technology of behavior' to improve human society. Many traditional values seem to be in the way of this desirable outcome, but Skinner believed in a sort of historical inevitability in science which ensures that they must give way before a behavioral analysis:

> In what we may call the prescientific view [Skinner adds disingenuously that 'the word is not necessarily pejorative'!] a person's behavior is at least to some extent his own achievement ... he is to be given credit for his successes and blamed for his failures. In the scientific view ... a person's behavior is determined by a genetic endowment traceable to the evolutionary history of the species and by the environmental circumstances to which as an individual he has been exposed. Neither view can be proved, but it is in the nature of scientific inquiry that the evidence should shift in favor of the second.[8]

Elsewhere Skinner attacks punishment, 'feelings' and above all the concept of what he calls 'autonomous man'. His attack on autonomy is at the core of his opposition to traditional morality:

> Two features of autonomous man are particularly trouble-some. In the traditional view, a person is free. He is autonomous in the sense that his behavior is uncaused. He can therefore be held responsible for what he does and justly punished if he offends. That view, together with its associated practices, must be re-examined when a scientific analysis reveals unsuspected controlling relations between behavior and environment.[9]

These passages lead us up two garden paths at once. First, we are led to believe that science will inevitably identify more and more environmental causes for human behavior. Behavior will become more and more predictable. This is possible; it is far from inevitable. Secondly, the passages invite us to accept without scrutiny a questionable proposition: that as we understand better the environmental causes for behavior, we *must* attach less weight to the autonomy of the individual. Skinner wishes us to believe that if behavior is perfectly determined, the individual must lose all responsibility for his actions.

If this opposition between determinism and responsibility is false, then the conclusions that Skinner draws from it are also false. But the opposition allows him to devote much of *Beyond freedom and dignity* to systematic destruction of traditional values and views of man, confident that if traditional views fall, the rhetorical seesaw he has built will cause his own views to rise in the reader's estimation.

Continuing his attack on the idea of autonomy, Skinner points to historians' discussions of 'influences' in the lives of the great. He caricatures the conventional view thus: 'Autonomous man survives in the face of all this because he is the happy exception. Theologians [not a prestigious group among psychologists!] have reconciled predestination with free will ...' Skinner at least recognized that determinism and predestination are closely related, although determinism acts through genetics and personal history rather than through the agency of a Supreme Being. Skinner also admits that both determinism and predestination raise the specter of the free-will problem.

But he offers no arguments. He simply assumes a particular solution to the problem, namely that determinism precludes free will. He also assumes that conventional judicial practices, especially punishment for misdeeds, somehow depend upon the free-will assumption. All these assertions – perfect determinism, the implication that autonomy is a myth, and the supposed dependence of judicial practices on non-determinism – are either questionable or false.

Determinism and autonomy. Let's look first at determinism. Is it a fact? It clearly is not a fact *now*. At present, human behavior cannot be predicted with anything like the precision required. We may doubt whether determinism at the required level can ever be established. For the moment, we can certainly ignore many of Skinner's societal recommendations on the grounds that the knowledge of human behavior he presupposes does not exist. Nevertheless, we must admit that as science advances, our behavior may turn out to be predictable in detail by some super-psychology of the future. So we cannot avoid indefinitely the philosophical problem of reconciling determinism with traditional notions of freedom and responsibility. I believe that reconciliation is perfectly possible. Let's look at some of the arguments that dissolve the inverse linkage between behavioral determinism and individual responsibility that Skinner has set up.

Suppose, gentle reader, that a generous bond trader offers you a choice between two piles of money: one with ten dollars, the other with one thousand. Under almost any foreseeable set of circumstances, I predict that you will choose the one-thousand-dollar pile. This is the level of predictability that Skinner promises us we will eventually have for all behavior, not just choices between vastly disparate outcomes. So we can reasonably ask if, in this simple situation, your autonomy has been destroyed. The answer, surely, is 'obviously not' under any generally accepted notion of 'freedom'.[10] Another example: suppose you ask a mathematician 'What is the square root of 1024?' With perfect predictability he will answer '32'. Has his autonomy been destroyed? Again, obviously not. Why is it that in these concrete cases there seems to be no conflict between predictability and autonomy, yet most people who read Skinner's arguments end up being convinced there is a problem?

Skinner's opposition between freedom and predictability is

superficially persuasive because he tacitly conflates subject and object. Freedom is an entirely *subjective* concept – a man is free if he feels free.[11] A mathematician does not feel that the laws of arithmetic impinge on his freedom. Predictability (by oneself or others) is an *objective* property. It simply has no bearing on the feeling of freedom. The husband whose behavior is completely predictable by his wife is no less free than the husband whose wife is constantly surprised.

Assuming that he attaches some value to the 'feeling of freedom' a good behaviorist would go on and ask 'What are the environmental conditions that cause men to give expression to this feeling?' (When do men feel free?) This, of course, is precisely the subject matter of the 'literatures of freedom and dignity' that Skinner is at pains to disparage.[12]

Justice. But suppose we concede the point, suppose determinism is a fact, what then follows? At first blush, predictability of behavior does seem to raise issues of *justice*. If a man's criminal behavior is perfectly predictable from his personal history, punishment for wrongdoing may seem to be unjust. Defense attorneys will frequently argue that a man who was the child of abusive parents should not be held fully responsible for his assaultive actions as an adult, for example. The response to this argument rests on what we mean by 'just' and on the social purposes of punishment. (Skinner was happy to embrace such matters within radical behaviorism, at the cost of ignoring entire disciplines, such as jurisprudence, economics and moral philosophy.) For the moment, let's take a position that is behaviorist, but not Skinnerian, and argue that a punishment is 'just' if it serves the social purpose of minimizing human suffering. And suffering must of course comprise both the damage to society done by criminals and the damage to individual criminals done by just punishment.[13] Let's assume that that level of punishment (for a given crime) is optimal which minimizes the sum of these two costs.

Some legal scholars may find this definition too narrow. But it is perfectly consistent with Skinner's pragmatic approach to such problems. I will nevertheless argue that from this point of view, predictability of behavior should not prevent us from holding people responsible for their actions. On the contrary, without predictability, *no* social purpose would could served by the concept of personal responsibility.

What does 'holding a man responsible' for his actions mean? In practice it means nothing more than making him subject to punishment if he breaks the law. Why, then should Skinner object to the idea, which is obviously perfectly behavioristic? He objects for two reasons, neither valid: First, because responsibility implies the potential for *punishment*, to which he is universally opposed, supposedly on the grounds that it does not work very well. And secondly because he mistakenly assumes that personal responsibility rests on the idea of 'autonomous man', which he believed he had refuted. Let's look first at Skinner's arguments against punishment and then return to the supposed role of autonomous man in conventional judicial practices.

Is punishment bad? Punishment is termed by Skinner 'aversive control' and the one clear value that emerges from his writings is unequivocal opposition to it. He doesn't argue the case on moral grounds, of course, but on grounds of inefficacy: 'Reward and punishment do not differ merely in the direction of the changes they induce [there is in fact continuing debate in the technical literature about whether or not this is true] ... Punished behavior is likely to reappear after the punitive contingencies are withdrawn.'[14] Later on, he adds that another problem with aversive control is that it gives rise to 'counterattack'. People will fight attempts at aversive control. In place of punishment, Skinner advocates exclusive use of positive reinforcement, because it works better.

The fallacy in this argument is that the supposedly universal superiority of positive reinforcement over punishment is simply not a fact. Laboratory studies do *not* show that punishment is always less effective than reward. Indeed, under many conditions, punishment is quicker and more effective than reward. Parents of young children can attest – and laboratory experiments confirm – that it is easier and faster to eliminate unwanted behavior through punishment than by the indirect means (such as rewarding a competing behavior) required by positive methods. To Skinner's objection that the behavior returns when punishment is withdrawn there are two excellent replies: (a) Rewarded behavior also ceases when the reward is withdrawn. And (b) behavior that is maintained by what is called an *avoidance* schedule[15] is *much more* resistant to extinction when the aversive stimulus is withdrawn than behavior maintained by positive reinforcement. We cannot abandon the idea of personal responsibility on the pragmatic ground that punishment is ineffective.

What of 'counterattack', the bad side-effects of punishment? People do indeed try to evade or eliminate aversive contingencies. The criminal seeks to avoid punishment for his crime, oppressed citizens may revolt, the guilty suspect attacks the police officer.[16] The problem is that positive reinforcement also has undesirable side-effects. The ambitious student who does charitable work not in order to help poor people, but because it will look good on his *curriculum vitae*, the researcher who fakes his data in order to win a research grant, the financier who cheats widows and orphans to make a killing in the market, are all showing bad side-effects of positive reinforcement of one sort or another. Flatterers, the objects of their flattery, and spoiled children also attest to the ill effects of positive reinforcement.

The good Skinnerian will object at this point that the problem with the spoiled child is not excess of positive reinforcement, but a poor *schedule* of reinforcement. The child was rewarded for the wrong things. But of course the same argument can be offered for the violent man abused as a child: his problem may be not the punishment he received, but the fact that it was excessive and indiscriminate.

Even positive reinforcement may generate what Skinner calls 'countercontrol'. Some schedules of positive reinforcement, such as variable-ratio schedules, are very effective in generating responding at a high rate. As Skinner frequently points out, *piece work* (payment per item produced) is just such a schedule. Yet piece work notoriously generates strong countercontrol. Labor unions have universally condemned it, and the practice survives mainly in professions such as medicine, law, and trading in stocks and bonds where the reinforcers are inordinately large.[17]

An evolutionary argument for punishment. The ever-flexible Darwinian metaphor can be turned to the *support* of some measure of aversive control in the criminal-justice system. The argument is based on the idea of cultural evolution, and runs as follows. Darwin wrote: 'For natural selection acts by either now adapting the varying parts of each being to its organic and inorganic conditions of life; *or by having adapted them during past periods of time* ... .'[18] In other words, selection acts slowly and its effects are often delayed. Skinner would have to agree that we can substitute 'cultural practice' for 'being'. Like Darwin, he has argued that many evolved characteristics represent the effects of past selection. He has also made this argument for cultural features. We may also reasonably assume that although cultural selection is certainly faster than natural selection, it is a great deal slower than the behavioral selection within an individual's lifetime that we call learning.

The notion that selection acts slowly has an obvious bearing on the problem of the crime level. Most writers agree that the general level of crime in this century in Western nations (at least until recently) has been lower than in the previous centuries. There has probably been a secular reduction in lawlessness over the past several hundred years (although statistics for past centuries are sparse, so the evidence is far from conclusive). At the same time, the severity of punishment for all grades of crime has eased: we no longer imprison a child for stealing a loaf of bread, place a citizen in the stocks for debt, beat a youth for petty theft, or behead a man for speaking treasonably. Punishments have been reduced in other ways as well: the time lag between arrest and actual imposition of the penalty is much longer than it was a hundred or more years ago, especially in the US. Because of the frequent introduction of new measures to protect individual rights, the probability of punishment for crimes (even assuming that arrest probabilities have not changed) may also have decreased in recent decades. It is well accepted that increase in the delay, or reduction in the probability, of reinforcement or punishment, greatly diminishes their effects. Because the effects of cultural selection are slow, these reductions in the effectiveness of punishment may well take many years to have an effect. It is possible to argue, therefore, that the low level of lawlessness for most of this century is a delayed effect of the severe punishments meted out even to minor criminals in centuries past. Similarly, the apparent *increase* in crime in recent years may equally be a delayed response to the *relaxation* of penalties over the past fifty years.

Psychologists are almost unanimous in their opposition to punishment as a way of changing behavior. It is perhaps the *only* thing on which they agree. Skinner's clear opposition to punishment undoubtedly attracted liberal followers to views

71

that in other respects often appear totalitarian.[19] But examination of the experimental data shows that Skinner's objections to punishment are in fact ideological, not pragmatic. If the cultural-evolution argument is correct, the universal condemnation of punishment by psychologists may actually have contributed to the crime problem. If psychological opinion is believed, then every increase in crime will be interpreted by the political system as a failure of the 'old' methods (punishment).[20] Society's response to the increase will therefore be alleviation of punishment and the substitution of positive reinforcement. Because positive reinforcement is less effective than punishment in eliminating unwanted behavior, each alleviation will eventually produce an increase in crime, which will elicit calls for further alleviation, and so on. The result will eventually be a highly unstable situation with very high levels of crime – the situation in much of North America today.

I'm not sure whether this view of the societal effects of punishment is true or not. Human societies are complex beyond our imagination and it is rarely possible to be certain about the causes of any large social problem. Experiments cannot be done, and almost all positions are infused with ideology. Nevertheless, the argument for appropriate use of aversive control deserves to be discussed. I suspect that it is closer to the truth than Skinner's blanket condemnation.

Clearly, there are strengths and weaknesses to both punishment and positive reinforcement. Thus, conventional judicial practices cannot be abandoned on the grounds that punishment is uniquely ineffective. Is punishment immoral? Perhaps, but as we will see in the section below on 'Values', Skinner provides no basis for this belief. Skinner's case against the idea of personal responsibility thus rests entirely on his 'autonomous man' argument. How good is it?

'Autonomous man' and personal responsibility. 'Holding a man responsible' is nothing more than making him aware of the aversive contingencies that enforce punishment for misbehavior. Because human beings, unlike pigeons, can learn about contingencies without actually experiencing them (Skinner calls this *rule-guided* behavior, in contrast to the *contingency-governed* behavior of nonverbal animals), awareness of a punishing contingency will usually result in obedience to it. The aversive stimulus need never be experienced by the law-abiding

72

citizen. Thus, even if punishment is intrinsically undesirable, its actual use in civilized societies will usually be minimal and must be balanced against the common interest in a crime-free community. We cannot, therefore, condemn the idea of personal responsibility because it implies the possibility of punishment.

Personal responsibility also does not depend on Skinner's notion of 'autonomous man'. Skinner defines 'autonomy' as 'absence of causation'. There are philosophical problems with this idea, but even if it were true, the legitimacy of just punishment does not depend on it. The truth is precisely the opposite. It is precisely because people *are* sensitive to contingencies – their behavior *is* subject to causal influences – that punishment is used. If criminal behavior is predictably deterred by punishment, the justly punished criminal is less likely to disobey the law again, and serves as an example to other potential law-breakers. But if behavior were unpredictable and unaffected by contingencies – if it were uncaused, in Skinner's caricature of autonomous man – there would be absolutely no point to punishment (or any other form of behavioral control), because it would have no effect. Thus the idea of personal responsibility cannot be dismissed because behavior is determined or because punishment is ineffective.

These arguments suggest the proper treatment for our child-abused assaulter. Even if his assaultive behavior were partly determined by his unfortunate childhood – which cannot be proved now, and is likely to remain unprovable in such cases for generations to come – the infliction of punishment may still be appropriate. The fact that his past behavior was caused by something or other has absolutely no bearing on his present susceptibility to deterrence, or on the likelihood that others with similar histories will be deterred by observing the retribution that has been visited upon him. Indeed, if a person's criminal behavior can be traced to absence of appropriate and systematic punishment for bad behavior in the past, then punishment may well be what is needed now.

Only when punishment is likely to be completely *in*effective as a deterrent does the law quite properly limit its use. If the criminal is insane, or if injury was the unintended result of actions whose harmful outcome was unforeseeable, no guilt is attached to the perpetrator and no punishment is given –

because punishment can play no role in preventing the recurrence of such acts. The law is not an ass in all things.

Notice that this argument is strictly behavioristic. The behaviorist case for personal responsibility rests entirely on the beneficial *collective* effects of just punishment. It does not rest on philosophical notions of individual autonomy or personal morality, although such notions may play a role in training the young. Skinner was perhaps prevented from taking this line by two things: his deep-rooted and fundamentally irrational objection to punishment; and the fact that the arguments I have just made are close to arguments that are relatively commonplace in the literature of jurisprudence (see Box 4.1). By abandoning his objections to punishment, Skinner would have destroyed much of the uniqueness of his position.

Box 4.1

I deny not the existence of mental phenomena but the utility for law of the concept of mind in which intentions and free will figure. 'The division of acts into some for which a man is regarded as responsible, and others for which he is not, is part of the social apparatus of reward and punishment: responsibility is allocated where rewards and punishments have tended to work as incentives and deterrents.'[21] And being social rather than philosophical in purpose, the allocation of responsibility need not follow the division between free and coerced acts. A person who ... kills in self-defense is excused from criminal liability, but not the killer who would not have killed had he not been raised in a poor home by harsh parents. (Richard Posner)

Values

Skinner devotes an entire chapter in *Beyond freedom and dignity* to *values*. He was well aware that people would look to his philosophy for a guide to 'the good'. He provides none, other than to equate 'good' with positive reinforcement and 'bad' with punishment: '... the only good things are positive reinforcers, and the only bad things are negative reinforcers.'[22] This is unhelpful if we are not given some independent guide to what is reinforcing. Unfortunately the set of all possible reinforcers, for a pigeon much less a human being, cannot be specified in advance. Philosophers have made the same point: even the most careful observation of how people actually behave fails to discover any rule that will permit us to deduce 'all and only' things that they all call 'good'.[23] Morality cannot be deduced from nature.

The problem is that even the most exhaustive study of what people actually do must fail to provide us with a guide to what they should do. This confusion of what *is* with what *should be* is the main problem with Skinner's approach to values. Skinner's rather diffident attempt to get out of this box is evolutionary: 'Things are good (positively reinforcing) or bad (negatively reinforcing) presumably because of the contingencies of survival under which the species evolved.' His way out of the trap is to propose 'survival' – of the culture or the species – as a superordinate value from which all others can be deduced. It is hard to quarrel with this position in the abstract. Few would defend a belief or custom that is bound to cause the downfall of the culture that gives rise to it. The problem with 'survival' as a value is that it is what I will call a 'Nostradamus' criterion, and provides little or no practical guidance. Skinner's descriptive approach to values gets him into a second difficulty. Because he is reluctant to define 'reinforcers' in advance he often assumes that they are mostly set by the history of the species, and are not alterable within a man's lifetime.

It is not plausible that all reinforcers are innate, nor is it reasonable to assume that the ill-defined mechanism of conditioned reinforcement is sufficient to account for those reinforcers that are clearly acquired. This approach (termed primary and secondary drives) was tried by Hull and other early behaviorists and abandoned. It is simply not possible to link all rewards to a few inherited ones by this mechanism – or at least, no one has done so convincingly. It may be reasonable to assume that sex, hunger, thirst, perhaps even things like a love of music, are entirely innate. And clearly, 'neutral' stimuli may be linked to these motives through conditioning principles. There is a character in the *Tale of Genji*, for example, who is erotically stimulated by the calligraphy of his beloved – an example of Pavlovian conditioning, no doubt. It is much less plausible to assume that being reinforced by a red sports car, James Joyce or a particular brand of sneaker can be linked in this way with innate reinforcers.

Defenders of Skinner will argue that he never took the conditioned-reinforcement position. Reinforcers are where you find them, according to Skinner. Well, yes – and no. In some places, Skinner loosely ties all reinforcers to primary reinforcement via the ideas of conditioned and generalized reinforcement. But in his later writings, he usually disclaimed any need to define the set of reinforcers. And as we have just seen, in *Beyond freedom and dignity* he comes out for an entirely Darwinian interpretation.

On still another tack, Skinner defines the words 'good' and 'bad' in terms of community practice: 'Behavior is called good or bad ... according to the way in which it is usually reinforced by others.'[24] This says little more than that 'good acts are what people call good, and bad acts are what they call bad', which is often true but not helpful. He might have gone on to say that many reinforcers are established socially (the favored sneaker brand, for example), but this would have led into sociological complexities which he always avoided. And the origin of this social behavior ('Why this brand of sneaker?' 'Why sneaker at all?') would still be unexplained.

If reinforcers are set for life, what is one to do when confronted with apparently undesirable reinforced behavior, such as excessive indulgence in recreational drugs? The Darwinian metaphor gives little guidance. If these substances formed part of our 'selection environment' then presumably this behavior, despite its apparent ill-effects, must have served some positive function. We should therefore leave it alone. If a drug is a new arrival, then these habits may now be maladaptive (Skinner discusses such cases). We should desist, Skinner would say, because their negative effects are so obvious.

The ultimate value he invokes here – the only one that is explicitly defended in his utopian writings – is 'survival of the culture'. Presumably, cultures addicted to alcohol and tobacco are less 'fit' (in the Darwinian sense) than cultures not so addicted. The problem with 'survival of the culture' as a value is that it requires a Nostradamus – perfect knowledge of the future – if it is to be a useful guide. It is as accurate, and as helpful, as the stock-market advice: 'Buy low, sell high.' While some customs, like indiscriminate homicide, are clearly maladaptive under all imaginable circumstances, others, like respect for parents, monogamy, tolerance, selflessness, the Divine Right of Kings, even a belief in a single objective reality, are more contingent. The problem is that most of the prescriptions of traditional morality fall in the latter class. We simply do not know, belief by belief, custom by custom, whether our culture would in the long run be better off with or without them. Yet some cultures are clearly more likely to survive than others. It seems very likely, moreover, that the ones that survive will have many beliefs that were in fact essential to their survival, but whose importance could not have been foreseen.[25]

There is a parallel in the evolution of animal species. All animals behave instinctively, to some degree. Much of human behavior, even, involves preferences and habits that owe little to experience. Indeed, it is hard to conceive of any adaptive entity that could succeed in the evolutionary race by relying entirely on learning. It seems certain, therefore, that a culture with some unquestioned, culturally inherited, beliefs is fitter[26] than a culture with none or only a few. Apparently we should take *some* things on faith. But which things? Here, alas, evolutionary epistemology provides no real guidance. Nevertheless, moralists can take some comfort from this argument, which constitutes a scientific argument for faith – if not for any faith in particular.[27]

Summary: Skinner's morality

In *Beyond freedom and dignity* Skinner undermines many traditional beliefs. He offers nothing as substitutes but Nostradamus and a rejection of aversive control. G.K. Chesterton says somewhere that those who do not believe in God believe not in nothing, but in anything. Less theistically, we can say that those who lack any inherited system of beliefs are more susceptible to persuasion. If modern media-dominated societies are adept at anything, it is persuasion, to which whole industries and many of our best minds are devoted. It is not an accident that children who grow up in homes where traditions are weak – the children of the underclass in the US, of Essex man in the UK, and of the workaholic nouveau riche everywhere – live by the values of commercial advertising. The intellectual classes have also abandoned most traditional beliefs – often for no better reason than that groups they oppose (religious fundamentalists, for example) support them. It is rational, not reactionary, to view the replacements with some suspicion. As tradition collapses, we should not be surprised to find the world overtaken by values that have not been tested by time. Many will surely, in time, turn out to be pernicious. Thus, I believe that by his attacks on traditional beliefs Skinner may have actually increased the amount of superstition in the world, not reduced it.

Mental life

His view of mental life is what distinguishes Skinner's radical behaviorism from the methodological behaviorism of his predecessors:

> Methodological behaviorism and certain versions of logical positivism could be said to ignore consciousness, feelings and states of mind, but radical behaviorism does not thus 'behead the organism'; it does not 'maintain a strictly behavioristic methodology by treating reports of introspection merely as verbal behavior'; and it was not designed to 'permit consciousness to atrophy'. What it has to say about consciousness is this: (a) Stimulation arising inside the body plays an important part in behavior. (b) The nervous systems through which it is effective evolved because of their role in the internal and external economy of the organism. (c) In the sense in which we say that a person is conscious of his surroundings, he is conscious of states or events in his body; he is under their control as stimuli ... a person may continue to talk, 'unconscious of the effect he is having on his listeners' if that effect is not exerting control on his behavior. Far from ignoring consciousness in this sense, a science of behavior has developed new ways of studying it.[28]

Skinner's view of mental life is probably the most obscure part of his writings. Let's take first his notion of internal stimulation, which he invokes to explain 'feeling' and 'thinking'. For example, when we answer the question 'What are you thinking? ... it is ... likely that we are describing private conditions associated with public behavior but not necessarily generated by it.'[29] What this seems to mean is that 'we' are describing some internal state (but the word 'state' is avoided in favor of 'stimulation') that normally goes along with speech but on this occasion occurs in the absence of speech. There are problems here that I can describe but cannot begin to elucidate. Who is observing this internal state? Since the state is internal, it presumably also includes some part of the observer, who is thus observing himself. And how are we to deal with an internal stimulus that we cannot see or measure? Skinner does not deal with these problems, and when confronted directly with them could not clarify his argument so that this writer, at least, could understand him.[30]

Skinner's position, obscure as it is, does give a plausible account of some aspects of mental life, such as pain and reports of internal disorders. Reports of pain, particularly when referred to sites within the body, are notoriously inaccurate. Heart-attack victims, for example, may report one or more of the following symptoms: pains in the left arm, the neck, even the back, as well as in the chest. Psychologist Edwin Boring years ago stimulated his own oesophagus and found that the place where he located the sensation was much closer to the mouth than the actual stimulus. On the other hand, people can report the location of a touch on the skin, particularly the skin of the hands or face, with great accuracy. Why this difference? Skinner gives a social answer: internal stimuli are reported inaccurately because the 'verbal community' cannot differentially reinforce accurate responding. A mother can only guess at the source of her child's 'tummy-ache'; neither child nor mother knows for sure. But if little Billy has fallen and grazed his knee, both know the source of the trouble very well. Since both know where the pain is, the mother can teach the child the proper label.

Skinner's account may be part of the truth. But children need no extrinsic reinforcement to locate a painful external stimulus. The evolutionary reason is that accurate location of the problem is essential to effective action. The animal that pricks its right paw but withdraws the left is a poor bet in the evolutionary race. Such specificity is much less important in the internal milieu. If identifying the sources of internal problems were of consequence to natural selection, no doubt we would locate them with accuracy also, and also without need for extrinsic reinforcement

—just as the mayfly innately knows its own kind and the song sparrow sings without instruction. The big difference between internally and externally caused distress is that little can be done to remove the source of internal distress. In the past, at least, nothing much hinged on accurate identification of internal problems, so that selection pressure for accuracy has been weak. As medical science offers more possibilities for corrective action, it constitutes a selection pressure favoring patients who can report the site of internal problems accurately. Individuals with atypical symptoms for cardiac problems or an inflamed appendix are at a slightly higher risk of dying than the population at large. After many generations, even such a small selective effect may produce noticeable changes in the population. A future generation may report cardiac ischemia with perfect accuracy. I suspect that weak selection pressure, rather than inaccessibility to social reinforcement, is a more likely explanation for inaccuracy in reporting internal events.

Skinner prefers to label something like 'seeing an object' or 'hearing a tune' as a 'response' rather than as a stimulus or a state. This allows him to deal with 'images' and 'hallucinations' as 'responses', different from seeing real objects only in that the objects happen to be absent: 'After hearing a piece of music several times, a person may hear it when it is not being played, though probably not as richly or as clearly. So far as we know, he is simply doing in the absence of the music some of the things he did in its presence.'[31] There can be little doubt that a person who is 'imagining' an object is in a state similar to his state when actually seeing the object (new evidence from brain-activity scans shows that visual areas of the brain are indeed active when the subject is 'seeing' an image, for example). Skinner's view is undoubtedly a useful antidote to the 'copy' theory of perception which asserts that 'imagining' an object actually recreates a 'mental picture' of the object. There is only weak evidence for the copy theory, and Skinner is right to point out that the assumption is unnecessary.[32] There is a problem with identifying a 'mental image' as a 'response', however, because the whole point about an image is that it is compatible with a whole set of potential responses, and an open-ended set at that. Thus, the person who sees an image of an apple might say 'I see an apple'; but he might also answer 'Yes' when asked 'Do you see what fell on Newton's head', or 'Are you thinking that one a

80

day may keep the doctor away?' In short, the *object* property of the image is lost when it is reduced to a response. Of course, Skinner was aware of all this, and dealt with it by evolving very flexible concepts of 'response' and 'stimulus'. It is this sort of elusiveness that allows Skinnerians to deny that their hero is a stimulus-response theorist – at the same time that a literal reading of what he says allows non-Skinnerians to assert that a stimulus-response theorist is precisely what he is.

*

B.F. Skinner was a brilliant experimenter. He invented the Skinner box, which is now the standard way of studying learned behavior in psychology and neurobiology. He reintroduced the psychology of learning to the individual after many years when most psychologists dealt with data only from groups. He showed that behavior can be studied directly, that it need not be viewed through the 'dark glass' of inferential statistics. He and his students went on to use the techniques he had invented to study reinforcement schedules, where they discovered a completely unsuspected sensitivity of operant behavior to the pattern and scheduling of intermittent reinforcers. This project revealed surprising similarities in behavior across species and has led directly to an important nexus between psychology, economics and behavioral ecology. Skinner provided a conceptual framework for understanding learning that (I believe) has yet to be fully explored – even though his strictures against theory prevented him from exploiting it himself and impeded the efforts of others to do so.

Skinner's work continues to have a substantial impact in applied areas, particularly clinical psychology, where it is known as 'behavior modification' or 'applied behavior analysis'. These methods are perhaps the *only* psychotherapeutic techniques whose efficacy (in a limited domain) has been conclusively proved. Largely through the work of Fred Keller, Skinner's ideas have also had significant effects on education.

No matter what criticisms are legitimately leveled at Skinner, he will always deserve credit for his emphasis on the *environment*. Much of his hostility to psychological concepts like 'feeling', the 'inner man', 'attitudes' and the like, was because these notions distract attention from the real causes[33] of behav-

81

ior, which lie in a person's past history. Moreover, these are causes we can actually do something about. Attitude, no matter how precisely measured, predicts actual behavior imperfectly. It is notorious that no man can know if he is capable of heroism until he finds himself in a situation where heroism is required. Who has not changed his voting preference at the last minute? Who has not behaved in a more (or less) prejudiced way than expected in a real-life context. 'Attitude' is a snapshot; but behavior is a movie. Most psychologists are happy to deal with 'attitudes', rather than historical causes, not just because attitudes are easy to measure (there is a massive industry of test-makers, focus-group organizers and opinion pollsters who make attitude-measurement their business), but because attitudes seem like easy-to-change things. A person's individual history, on the other hand, extends over many years. His behavior and his attitudes develop over time in response to all sorts of social and intellectual influences in ways that depend on his own changing constitution. These complex effects are hardly understood at all. Modifying behavior that grows out of such an environmental history may in fact be very difficult (if you doubt it, just look at 'attitudes' in Northern Ireland or the Balkans). Nevertheless, the environment is where psychologists *must* look if they are to understand normal human behavior. Every area of applied psychology would be farther along if Skinner's admonition to 'keep your eye on the environment' had been followed more conscientiously.

Skinner spent the last twenty years of his life engaged almost exclusively in writing about radical behaviorism and society. It was perhaps inevitable that these writings should go very far beyond experimental data and theoretical understanding. They reveal a hidden ideology – his opposition to aversive control – that forced Skinner to create a number of fallacious arguments.[34] Most significantly, his ideology prevented him from following through on his own behavioristic premises. It is hard to avoid the impression that in *Beyond freedom and dignity* Skinner is 'mistaking the finger for the moon' – attacking conventional views of man when the real problem is the inconsistency between his own unexamined beliefs and the facts of behavior revealed through the methods he had himself invented. A great scientist wrote:

4. Radical Behaviorism and Society

Science is a willingness to accept facts even when they are opposed to wishes. Thoughtful men have perhaps always known that we are likely to see things as we want to see them instead of as they are ... Scientists have simply found that being honest – with oneself as much as with others – is essential to progress ... Scientists have also discovered the value of remaining without an answer until a satisfactory one can be found.[35]

Although these words are Skinner's, in his later writings he failed to follow them. It is scant comfort that his sin in this respect is no greater than the sins of all those other over-confident social scientists – psychologists, psychiatrists, sociologists, economists – who continue to go beyond their narrow, particular and often ideologically driven understandings of human nature and society in 'expert' testimony of all kinds. They should keep silent, or at least show a decent modesty in the face of our enormous ignorance. Human nature is stranger than we know – and stranger even than we can imagine. In vital matters like marriage, raising children, and the punishment of crime it will be many, many, years before the one-dimensional pronouncements of 'experts' can be reliably trusted over traditional wisdom and personal experience.

Mind and Mechanism: Behaviorism Today

Where have all the behaviorists gone? In 1976, it was possible to write: '... since the days of Chicago functionalism and Columbia Thorndikianism, no one has seriously doubted the hegemony of behaviorism in American psychology. So-called cognitive psychology, considered by many the only viable option to behaviorism, has, in fact, existed more by contrast with behaviorism than as a school of thought in its own right.'[1] Yet shortly thereafter, the 'cognitive revolution' displaced behaviorism from psychology's front page and, increasingly, from departments of psychology across the land. What happened?

What happened was that psychologists got leave to 'do what comes naturally' – leave denied to them by the behaviorism of Watson and his successors for more than sixty years. What comes naturally to psychologists is *mentalism*. 'Psychology is the science of mental life' said William James in 1890.[2] Not only do psychologists want to study mental life, they want to study the mental life of *human beings*. This was also impeded by the behaviorists, who argued from evolutionary biology that simpler, hence more comprehensible, antecedents of the human mind are to be found in the minds of animals. The need for experiments in which reward and punishment may be freely administered also implied that scientific psychology must be centered on animal experiments, soon to be dismissively termed 'rat psychology'. Psychologists had been chafing against the constraints of biology and behaviorism for two generations when they were liberated by the new 'cognitive revolution'. The new cognitive psychology legitimated the study of language, mental representation and consciousness which (it was argued) had been ruled out or trivialized by the old behaviorism. As one apostle of the cognitive revolution wrote recently:

> ... the sole purpose of science is not to frame parsimonious laws. Notwithstanding Watson's and Skinner's emphasis on the prediction and control of behavior, science aims to *explain* phenomena, not merely to describe them in laws. And explanations, of course, take the form of theories. Hence, if mental states exist, a complete psychological explanation should give an account of them even if they could be dropped from the laws of behavior.[3]

How was this emancipation achieved? Chiefly through two things: the digital computer, and the act of theoretical *seppuku* committed by Skinnerian radical behaviorism.

The digital computer meant that theories – of mental life, perception, syntax or whatever – could now be *simulated*, made up into a working model, programmed on a computer. This was heady stuff in the 1960s and 1970s. Nobel-laureates-to-be boasted that the best chess player in the world would be a computer within ten years, automatic language translation was around the corner, and comprehensive models of thought were on the horizon. Already, in 1957, a computer program had discovered novel proofs for theorems in Russell and Whitehead's *Principia mathematica*.[4] The horizon seemed both limitless and close at hand.

Not only did computation offer power, it also offered respectability. Rigor and quantification had been almost a monopoly of the behaviorists. The vague, verbal theorizing of the Gestalt psychologists and other proto-cognitive psychologists could easily be dismissed. But now, the ability to simulate mentalistic theories with perfect precision conferred a sort of Good Housekeeping Seal of Approval on cognitive psychology. No longer need cognitive psychologists feel embarrassed by hard-headed behaviorists. Philosophical objections to the study of consciousness remained unanswered, but no matter: computers could remember, perceive, even understand. The possibilities appeared boundless. They are not. Now, with computers on every desktop greater in power by a factor of a hundred or more than the water-cooled monsters available to the prophets of cognitive science,[5] the prospects no longer seem so rosy.

Radical behaviorists were insulated from the siren song of cognitivism by Skinnerian suspicion of formal theory and by their dedication to experimental data as an end in itself. Behaviorists trained in the traditions of Hull and Tolman were much more susceptible, however. Several of the leading cognitive psychologists of the 1970s and 1980s are retreaded rat-runners, or at least, people reared in the Hullian tradition. The few neo-Tolmanians for the most part embraced with enthusiasm the new animal-cognition movement, described earlier in Chapter 1.

Cognitivism in crisis

How has the computer-assisted excitement of the original cognitivists panned out? Attacks are coming from the left and the right. On the left, philosophers are arguing that cognitivism is failing because the computer metaphor is wrong – and because cognitivism is not mental enough. On the right, some artificial intelligence (AI) researchers and roboticists are arguing that the emphasis on symbolic thought is largely irrelevant to the development of truly intelligent systems. I believe that the philosophical objections to contemporary cognitive psychology merely underscore the importance of a sophisticated behaviorism. The AI objections partly define the new behaviorism. Let's look at the philosophy first.

Philosophical objections to cognitive psychology. John Searle has mounted the most organized attack on mainstream cognitive psychology. He objects to its central tenet: that the brain is like a computer and cognitive operations like a program running on that computer.[6] Searle's main objection is that *anything* can be conceived of as a computer: a ball rolling down an inclined plane, for example, is an analogue computer that computes Newton's laws of motion; a nail driven into a plank computes the distance it must travel given the force of the hammer and the friction of the wood. The problem, says Searle, is that computational properties are not intrinsic to any system; they are interpretations imposed from outside.

Searle's second objection is to accuse cognitivism of the familiar homunculus fallacy. Sophisticated cognitivists are of course aware of this problem: there is no 'little man in the head' looking at some sort of screen on which the products of sensation are

---

Box 5.1. The varieties of cognitivism

Just to keep the terminology straight, I call the view that all there is to having a mind is having a program, Strong AI, the view that brain processes (and mental processes) can be simulated computationally, Weak AI, and the view that the brain is a digital computer, cognitivism. (John Searle)[7]

---

displayed. Nevertheless, the ways in which important problems are presented imply such a little man, says Searle: 'Typical homunculus questions in cognitive science are such as the following: "How does the visual system compute shape from shading; how does it compute object distance from size of retinal image?" '[8] The savvy cognitivist might respond by saying that what is really meant is 'How is information about object distance represented in the brain?' and 'How is this information derived from the retinal input?' He will need to add, of course, 'How do we know these things?' In other words, we need to know something about how states of mind are translated into things we can measure, i.e. into behavior.

This response shows that the question of representation cannot be separated from the questions of computation and action – but it often is, as Searle's questions show. When all three are considered together, it is difficult to see how they amount to asking more than 'How does the brain work to make behavior?' which is not necessarily a computational or even a cognitive question.

Searle's case against the computer metaphor for the mind seems solid, and much of the standard cognitivist boilerplate about 'information processing' and computational 'levels' dissolves under his analysis. No information is being processed, perhaps nothing is being 'represented': the external world is changing, neurons are firing, chemicals are circulating and physical actions are occurring. The psychologist's job is to find the connections among these events. My own conclusion is that rhetoric about functional, hardware, computational and intentional 'levels' is empty in the absence of clear evidence of demarcation lines – which can come only from a truly comprehensive theoretical system that explains behavior within a level and connects levels to one another. There is as yet no 'mental chemistry' and 'mental physics' to provide justification for a division between 'atomic' and 'molecular' levels, for example. Hence, psychology is under no compulsion to accept these 'mental strata'.

There are other cognitive conceits that Searle might have attacked. One of the most egregious is the curious distinction between *competence* and *performance*. Like the set of 'levels' just discussed, this is another 'trust me' distinction that depends for its validity on the reader's acceptance of the proposer's view of the subject. The subject in this case is language, and the proposer is mathematical linguist Noam Chomsky.[9] The distinction is less conspicuous now than it used to be, but the kind of thinking it represents still permeates cognitive psychology. The idea is that language follows certain syntactic 'rules', but that actual examples – speech as she is spoke or writing as she is writ – fall short of perfection because of constraints such as memory limitations.

The arbitrariness of this distinction is obvious from a thought experiment. Suppose someone gives you a device of unknown function with a numerical keypad. You try it out by typing in various combinations, and you get the following set of outputs: 2*2=4, 20*20=400, 25*25=625, 30*30=900. 'Great!' you think. 'I've figured it out. It's a calculator that multiplies.' But then you try: 40*40=999 – whoops! It turns out that the calculator multiplies fine, so long as the answer is less than 1,000. Anything greater, and it just gives the largest number of which it is capable: 999. How shall we describe the behavior of this device? The competence-performance people would say, 'Well, the deep rule underlying this behavior is multiplication, but because of memory limitations, answers greater than 999 cannot be produced.' There is an exactly parallel argument in linguistic theory to account for the fact that people are limited in their ability to understand and produce deeply embedded, but perfectly grammatical, sentences. 'Fine', you may well say. 'What's wrong with the competence-performance account of the behavior of this "constrained" calculator?' The answer is 'Nothing, so far.' The problem is that there are alternative accounts, but that decision among them demands additional information.

For example, one alternative is that the device doesn't multiply at all, but rather just consults a fixed lookup table which comprises all the three-digit (or fewer) products of two-digit numbers. A 'brain lesion' (i.e. damage to the device memory) would support this view if it simply knocked out certain answers, but left others involving the two multiplicands unaffected. More general effects might support the competence-performance alternative. The point is that the competence-performance idea, which implies an organization involving a rule-following engine limited by memory and other constraints, represents just one kind of model for what is happening in the linguistic black box. We are under no obligation whatever to accept it without knowing both the exact nature of the rules that are being enforced and the precise constraints that limit their output. Without the details, we are simply invited to accept as a matter of fact what is nothing more than a self-imposed limitation on theoretical inquiry.

AI objections to cognitivism. John Searle ends his attack on cognitive psychology by writing: 'One of the unexpected consequences of this whole investigation is that I have quite inadvertently arrived at a defense ... of connectionism. Among their other merits, at least some connectionist models show how a system might convert a meaningful input into a meaningful output without any rules, principles, inferences or other sorts of meaningful phenomena in between. This is not to say that existing connectionist models are correct ... But it is to say that they are not obviously false or incoherent in the way that traditional cognitivist models ... are.'[10] *Connectionism* is the name adopted by theorists who use simplified models of nerve cells (neurons) and their connections to simulate behavior such as learning, pattern identification, associative memory and (the example Searle had in mind) the perception of grammatical regularities such as the rule for plural forms. The elements in such an account, the neurons and their connections, are completely un-mental and unintelligent.

This theme, intelligence through the collective action of many unintelligent agents, has been carried forward by researchers in *robotics*, the engineering of intelligent, autonomous artificial creatures. Robotics researcher Rodney Brooks, recently wrote critically of the current state of cognitive science:

No one talks about replicating the full gamut of human intelligence any more. Instead we see a retreat into specialized subproblems, such as ways to represent knowledge, natural language understanding, vision or even more specialized areas ... I ... believe that human level intelligence is too complex and little understood to be correctly decomposed into the right subpieces at the moment ... .we will never understand how to decompose human level intelligence until we've had a lot of practice with simpler level intelligence.[11]

He concludes, perhaps cynically, 'Representation has been the central issue in artificial intelligence work over the last 15 years only because it has provided an interface between otherwise isolated modules and conference papers.'

So, the latest word from the cognitive-science frontier seems to be that the standard AI approach has stalled. To get psychology moving again, it looks as if we might do better to return to simpler systems – to animals. Behaviorism and animal research may be on the way back, after all.

Brooks provides a plausible biological argument for this position. He notes that language, and symbolic communication generally, are very recent arrivals on the evolutionary scene. Most of evolutionary time was taken up developing creatures that could simply find their way about. Distinctively human abilities like speech and writing arrived only during the last few ticks of the evolutionary clock. 'This suggests that problem-solving behavior, language, expert knowledge and application, and reason, are all pretty simple once the essence of being and reacting are available ... This part of intelligence is where evolution has concentrated its time – it is much harder.'[12] It is perhaps no accident that the abilities that are hardest to simulate – motor coordination, object perception, the survival skills necessary to sustenance and reproduction – are the ones over which evolution labored longest.

Brooks' colleague at MIT, Pattie Maes, has summarized the conflict between old- and new-style AI as 'Knowledge-based vs. behavior-based artificial intelligence'.[13] 'Knowledge-based' AI is just the engineering equivalent of mainstream, symbolic, cognitive psychology. The fundamental concept for both knowledge-based AI and cognitive psychology is the idea of *representation*. The working assumption is that once you get the representation right, you have solved the problem – either of artificial intelligence, or of human cognition. 'Behavior-based' AI is a new development which denies both these ideas.[14] It argues instead that complex behavior arises from the combined actions of a multiplicity of stupid agents. There is no special internal representation of the external world. Or, at least, the representation is a by-product of the unintelligent action of more or less independent, simple processes. Slowly, as the advances from the old approach begin to slow and those from the new begin to accelerate, a new behaviorism, combining ideas from psychology, biology and engineering, is beginning to crystallize around these ideas.

It is still too early to know whether the arguments for a behavior-based approach are valid. What does seem clear is that the commitment of the early behaviorists to research on animals was abandoned prematurely. Cognitive science has enjoyed the usual 'high' induced by the appearance of a new technology (the digital computer). A few years earlier operant conditioning was comparably energized by the technology of the Skinner box and schedules of reinforcement. But the most recent advances in the study of cognition have come from artificial neural networks, a technology explicitly derived from biology and completely congenial to classical behavioristic associationism, if not to atheoretical radical behaviorism.[15]

The irony is that work on neural nets *should* have emerged from behaviorism, not cognitive psychology. The idea of stimulus-response associations was central to early behaviorism, and a network merely adds internal 'nodes' that can be associated with one another, as well as with external stimuli and responses. In the 1960s and 1970s a few attempts were made to extend neural-network ideas to rat-runner data,[16] but the antitheoretical bias of the radical behaviorists proved too strong and, in the end, neural-net ideas found more fertile ground among cognitive psychologists.

Connectionism is the name that Edward Thorndike gave to his approach to reinforcement learning more than seventy years ago. The same name has been independently adopted by contemporary proponents of parallel-processing techniques loosely derived from the properties of real nerve cells. But the new connectionists are generally unaware that their field is an example of what the biologists call convergent evolution: a return to an earlier form via a different evolutionary path.

Not a few traditional cognitive psychologists are properly un-easy about these new developments, which they correctly per-ceive as a resurrection of behaviorism under a new guise. Connectionism has therefore had a mixed reception, with many cognitive psychologists attempting to prove that connectionist systems are incapable of modeling one or more of the 'higher mental processes' that interest them.[17] None of these refuta-tions has stuck. Let's take a look at some of the ingredients of the new behaviorism.

Contemporary behaviorisms

The clearest division within contemporary behaviorism is be-tween those who continue to believe in a fundamentally pur-posive (teleological) approach to reinforcement learning, and those with a renewed commitment to behavioral mechanisms. I believe that the division is not fundamental. The teleologists are pessimists. They believe that the true behavioral or physi-ological mechanisms for behavior are so complex that we will never be able to unravel them in detail. On the other hand, behavior is adaptive and more or less goal-oriented. We can therefore understand it (they argue) by understanding its goals: how they are weighed and how the subject's strategies for attaining them are constrained. This view is quite close to folk psychology, the nonscientific way we attempt to understand the 'motives' of our spouses, children and colleagues.

Teleological behaviorism

Howard Rachlin has provided the most developed statement of teleological behaviorism (see Box 5.2). Rachlin's ideas are an explicit blend of some aspects of Skinner with some aspects of Aristotle. Although couched in terms of individual acts, tele-ological behaviorism defines 'response', 'stimulus' and 'rein-forcement' (the behavioristic trinity) in temporally extended terms that go well beyond their usual definitions: 'Skinner's original concept of reinforcement [is expanded] from a single event dependent on a single operant [response] (for example, a single food-pellet delivery immediately after a single lever press) to a pattern of environmental events perhaps only vaguely contingent on an overlapping pattern of operants.'[18]

The Aristotelian elements are the notion of teleology itself, a rejection (*contra* Skinner) of the private nature of mental events and the equation (*pro* Skinner) of mental states with action: 'For Aristotle, imagining was acting and not dreaming: vividness of imagination was not vividness of interior image but of overt behavior.'[19] The *final causes* in the system are the economist's utility functions, discovered through behavioral methods. The scheme is therefore very close to the economic idea of bounded rationality (see Chapters 2 & 3), and is thus open to many of the objections to rationality discussed earlier.

Box 5.2

Efficient-cause psychology is designed to answer the question of how a particular act is emitted; final-cause psychology is designed to answer the question of why a particular act is emitted ... final-cause psychology, a development of Skinnerian behaviorism, is ... called teleological behaviorism. (Howard Rachlin)[20]

Teleological behaviorism, like Watsonian behaviorism and (according to Rachlin) Aristotle, but unlike Skinner, rejects private events: 'If the individual himself reports "I have had the idea for some time but have only just recently acted upon it", he is describing a covert response which preceded the overt.'[21] For Aristotle, the idea would not be a covert response at all but a pattern of wholly overt responses including the individual's verbal report as one part of the pattern.[22] I will argue in a moment that this way of dealing with internal events as temporally extended patterns of stimuli and responses amounts to defining *internal states* in terms of equivalent histories.

The Darwinian metaphor. There is another way of looking at the problem of complex outcome-guided behavior that avoids the trap of rationalism implicit in the utility-function property of teleological behaviorism. The pessimist's alternative to what Rachlin calls 'efficient-cause' psychology is the Darwinian metaphor. If things are complicated, so that the search for mechanisms is futile, then the focus must be on selection, and the approach is close to Rachlin's or to classical microeconomics. But if we have some hope of understanding mechanisms, so that a causal account is possible, the emphasis is on variation: the mechanisms that generate behavior.

The Darwinian metaphor has practical consequences. Consider, for example, the problem of teaching a dull or depressed child who has simply 'given up'. Neither economics nor Skinnerian reinforcement-as-selection provides much help. The child is passive, hence there is no behavior and nothing from which to select. Reward is ineffective if the behavior on which it is contingent fails to occur. The economist's utility functions are empty if the behavior of the subject makes no contact with them. The point is to get *some* behavior. The Darwinian metaphor has some suggestions. Variation is increased by changing conditions, for example. 'Free' (i.e. response-independent) reinforcers generate a repertoire of behavior through Pavlovian mechanisms of variation discussed in Chapter 3. These treatments are simply what folk psychology would call 'encouraging the child' or 'raising his self-esteem'. But they are an improvement over folk psychology, because they entail a temporal order: *first* you encourage, *second* you reward more selectively. 'Self-esteem' is not an unqualified good, but a transitional state induced only to provide conditions that prepare the child to gain rewards by meeting objective criteria.

Box 5.3

Economics is the original theory of goal-directed choice. I shall argue that self-defeating behavior is best understood in terms of an economic marketplace within the individual ... the recent burgeoning of 'behavioral economics' has shown how nearly congruent reinforcement theory is with economics. (George Ainslie)[23]

A slightly different version of teleological behaviorism has been proposed by George Ainslie (see Box 5.3). His idea is that each individual acts not as a single, rational agent, but rather as a set of competing agents, each sensitive to the outcomes of the act it represents. The agents compete through a 'demon' that follows a version of Herrnstein's matching law (see Chapter 3) and chooses among them. The structure of Ainslie's system is not identical to the set of independent, stupid agents favored by the behavior-based AI people. It is perhaps closer to the distributed-cognition approach of AI guru Marvin Minsky in his 'society of mind'.[24] What does seem to be clear is that theorists of all persuasions seem to moving away from the idea of the person as a single executive decision maker towards parallel systems of more or less unintelligent entities that compete for control of overt behavior. I will return to this idea in a moment.

Theoretical behaviorism

The optimistic approach to behaviorism is to look for efficient causes: the antecedent factors that determine behavior and the mechanisms through which they act. Skinner was a qualified advocate of this view. He constantly emphasized the organism's *history* as the determinant of its behavior. Unfortunately, his emphasis was entirely on *reinforcement* history – he had no interest in nonreinforcement effects of great concern to other behaviorists such as latent learning, for example (see Chapter 1). Because he was uninterested in mechanism, Skinner also provided no way to interpret the effects of complex histories – no way for the effects of events in the remote past to combine with the effects of more recent events, for example. Perhaps for this reason, the experimental emphasis of single-organism research on operant conditioning has been overwhelmingly on what are known as *reversible* effects (see Chapter 2). For example, a pigeon might be trained for many experimental sessions to peck a key for food reinforcement on some intermittent schedule of food reinforcement. After twenty or more daily experimental sessions, its response rate, the average number of key pecks over an hour period, will stabilize at some value such as 65/minute. This value will be largely determined by the average rate (food deliveries/hour) at which the bird gets food, which in turn is determined by the parameters of the schedule (e.g. the average minimum interfood interval for a variable-interval schedule). The pigeon's rate of responding is largely independent of the bird's history prior to this particular protracted experimental condition. If the schedule parameter is changed, from 1 food delivery/minute to 2/minute, say, the bird will settle down at a higher peck rate, 75/minute, say. But if the schedule parameter is changed back again to 1/minute, the rate of pecking will eventually return to 65, its pre-change value.

Thus, the relation between schedule parameter and response rate is a *reversible* property of behavior. The problem is that the same behavior on these two occasions does not mean that the pigeon is in the same state. Behavior is often reversible; but the state of the organism rarely is. Hence, by restricting their attention to reversible properties of behavior, radical behaviorists avoided dealing with the deeply historical nature of learned behavior in higher organisms.

I will give just one example. Imagine an experimental situation with pigeons that involves not one but two response keys. Pecks on each key are paid off like a Las-Vegas-style one-armed bandit, probabilistically. Let's look at two different experimental histories. Pigeon A is trained at first to peck on the *left* response key and paid off on the probabilistic schedule; pecks on the *right* have no effect. After 50 or so reinforcements for pecking *left*, bird A is trained to peck only on the *right*; pecks on the *left* go unrewarded. After 300 reinforcements for *right* pecks (this might take four or five daily experimental sessions), pecks on neither key are rewarded (this is termed *extinction*). Pigeon B is trained throughout (350 reinforcements) to peck the *right* key only for food, then extinguished, like A.

There are two things to notice about this simple experiment: on the last day of rewarded training, the behavior of the two pigeons will be indistinguishable: both will be pecking exclusively on the *right* key. But in extinction, their behavior will be very different: Bird B, which has never got food for pecking *left*, will simply peck more and more slowly on the *right* until pecking ceases altogether. But Bird A, with its history of a few rewards for pecking *left*, will show some pecks to both keys before quitting entirely. What can this difference in behavior in extinction mean? If behavior is all that matters, the two birds were in the same state at the end of *right* training. So why did they behave differently when conditions changed?

There are two ways to deal with this divergence. The solution adopted by Rachlin is to redefine behavior in a temporally extended way. *Behavior* becomes *behavioral history*. Since our two pigeons have different histories, the fact that their response to a new condition (extinction) is not the same is no longer a puzzle. The problem with this view is that it provides no condensation of the data. It provides no rationale for similarities among histories. Not all histories produce the kind of divergence

5. Mind and Mechanism: Behaviorism Today

I have just described. It is possible, in principle and to some degree in practice, to group together histories that are *equivalent*, in the sense that the future behavior of the animal (in response to new conditions) will be the same after any history in the set. For example, in a version of the experiment I have described we might find that an animal with the history (number of rewards in parenthesis) *right*(10), *left*(10) behaves the same in extinction as an animal whose history is *left*(5), *right*(15), *left*(10). The usual way to describe this equivalence is to say that the two animals are in the same *state* after these two *equivalent histories*. The aim of the new *theoretical behaviorism*, therefore, is to understand the complete set of internal states of our animal, where each state is defined by a set of equivalent histories.[25]

Theoretical behaviorism (TB) is a natural descendant of both classical and Hullian behaviorism. It gets from classical behaviorism the conviction that we learn about the organism only through its behavior. It rejects, however, the view shared by Watson and Skinner that psychology need refer only to stimuli and responses. *Contra* Skinner, it argues that the skin does make a difference: events inside the organism (e.g. the changes wrought by past history) are *state* variables, not stimuli or responses. *Contra* cognitivism, internal states are not necessarily mental; *contra* Hullian behaviorism, internal states are not necessarily physiological.[26] TB sees internal states as purely theoretical constructions based on information from historical experiments. Nevertheless, it shares with Hullian behaviorism the idea that the ultimate aim of behavioral study is the derivation of *mechanisms* (and the expectation that these mechanisms will ultimately make some connection with brain physiology).[27]

Theoretical behaviorism is interested in mechanisms for entirely practical reasons. The argument runs like this: Classes of equivalent histories are defined by reference to potential experiments. But real animals are very complicated and historical experiments take time. There is no way that the full set of internal states of a real animal can be fully enumerated experimentally. Theoretical creativity is necessary, and theories arise not just from 'orderly arrangement of data', but also through invention. In practice, therefore, the main way to specify sets of equivalent histories is through dynamic theories that define how moment-by-moment experience changes the state of the organism. These theories can be compared with data, tested (if they do well enough with what is already known), overthrown (all theories are eventually overthrown), revised, and tested again, in the usual scientific way.

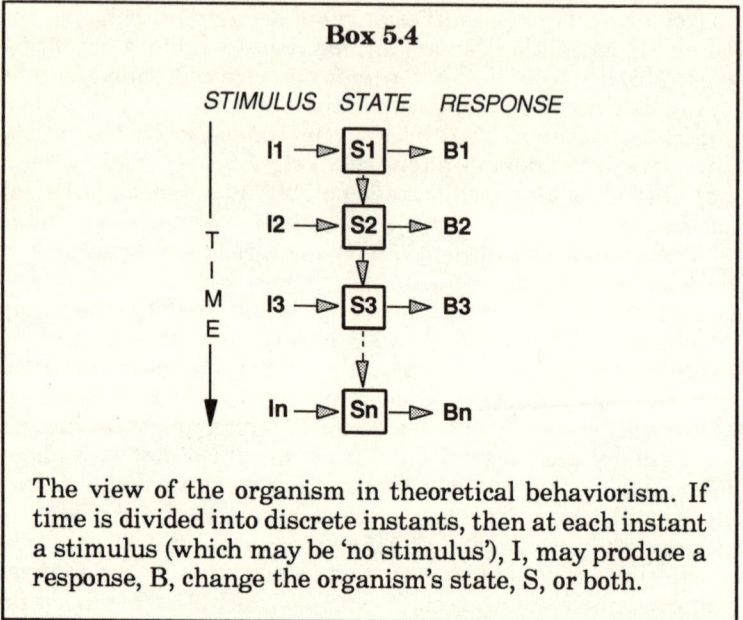

Box 5.4

STIMULUS   STATE   RESPONSE

$$I1 \rightarrow \boxed{S1} \rightarrow B1$$

$$I2 \rightarrow \boxed{S2} \rightarrow B2$$

T
I
M $$I3 \rightarrow \boxed{S3} \rightarrow B3$$
E

$$In \rightarrow \boxed{Sn} \rightarrow Bn$$

The view of the organism in theoretical behaviorism. If time is divided into discrete instants, then at each instant a stimulus (which may be 'no stimulus'), I, may produce a response, B, change the organism's state, S, or both.

How does theoretical behaviorism differ from cognitivism? Both are theoretical and both assume internal states. One difference is that theoretical behaviorism is explicitly historical and dynamic (see Box 5.4). It is not concerned directly with representation, but with the way that the organism is changed by its experience. A second difference is that theoretical behaviorism makes no presumptions about either its subject matter or its theoretical constructs. Cognitive psychology is 'the study of mental life'; TB is the study of the mechanisms of behavior, where *mechanism* is whatever works to account for behavior; and *behavior* is whatever can be usefully observed or measured, including reports of conscious experience (see below).[28] Theoretical behaviorism assumes in advance neither that the categories of consciousness are inevitable ingredients of any valid theory, nor that they must be immediately explicable by such a theory. 'Theories are where you find them' says TB; exploit whatever works. 'If consciousness comes out in the wash, fine; if not, no problem.'[29]

Box 5.5

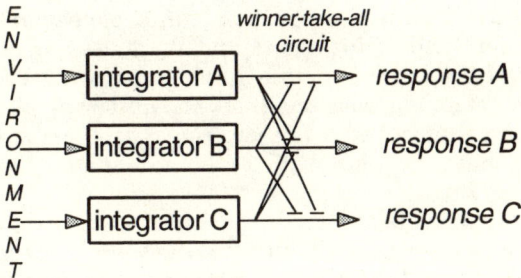

A popular class of behavioral models. Each is controlled by an 'integrator' that reflects its past history of payoff and has a certain 'strength'. These strengths compete for control of behavior, the strongest winning. Models of this type have been proposed for operant learning, habituation and discrimination reversal.

Box 5.4 just provides a framework. It tells us nothing about how stimuli and responses are to be defined. It does not specify the properties of the states: how many there are, the rules by which they change, and so on. These are the concern of specific theories and I refer the reader to technical sources for more details.[30] One emerging theme is illustrated in Box 5.5. It is the idea that many of the properties of simple learning can be explained by competition among independent agents ('integrators'), each of which retains a memory of its past effectiveness in a given context. We have already seen this theme in the earlier discussion of behavior-based AI. The 'state' of a model like this is just the set of 'strengths' of the integrators. The 'state-transition rules' are just the ways that these strengths change as the system behaves and encounters stimuli. Models along these general lines can account for the basic properties of operant learning, for some properties of complex choice, and for temporal properties of habituation, the progressive decrease in responding to repeated harmless stimulation.

Consciousness

Consciousness is a hot ticket in cognitive psychology these days. Respected foundations sponsor conferences on it; Nobel prizewinners aspire to understand it; philosophers and psychologists collaborate to define it.[31] 'There was a large measure of agreement among both scientists and philosophers at a recent symposium that not only is there a real problem of consciousness but that it is a scientific problem and that the time has come for scientists to tackle it.'[32]

Consciousness is the topic that most clearly differentiates behaviorists from nonbehaviorists. Just what scientific problems does it pose? How would a theoretical behaviorism attempt to answer them, and how would its answer differ from the answer offered by cognitive psychologists?

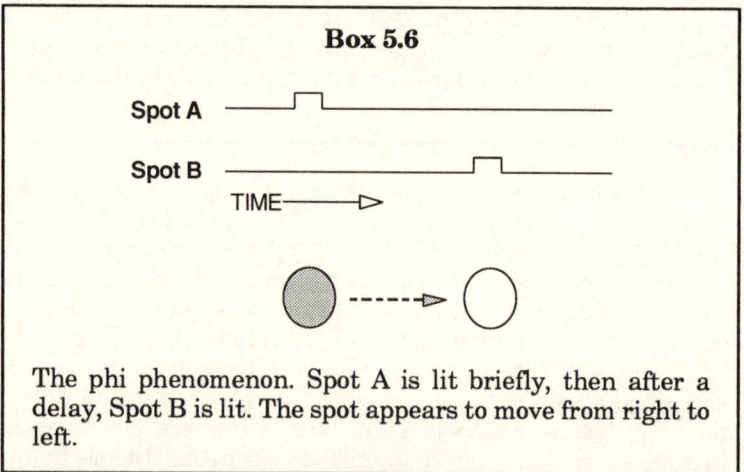

Box 5.6

The phi phenomenon. Spot A is lit briefly, then after a delay, Spot B is lit. The spot appears to move from right to left.

The cognitive approach can be illustrated by recent discussions of a perceptual effect known as the phi phenomenon. The phi phenomenon is the perceptual fusion of a succession of similar images flashed at brief intervals into the percept of a single moving image. When you watch a movie, your retina is stimulated 24 times each second with 24 static images. An object that takes up adjacent positions in each successive image is perceived as moving smoothly. The effect can be demonstrated experimentally with a single bright spot that is successively presented at one place and then at an adjacent place (see Box 5.6). There is a related effect in which the two spots are different colors. What is seen is a single moving spot which changes color at about the midpoint of its travel. The puzzles posed by this effect are discussed by philosopher Daniel Dennett and psychologist Marcel Kinsbourne, as follows:

> [Nelson] Goodman wondered: 'How are we able ... to fill in the spot at the intervening place-times along a path running from the first to the second flash *before that flash occurs?*' ... Unless there is precognition, the illusory content cannot be created until *after* some identification of the second spot occurs in the brain. But if this identification of the second spot is already 'in conscious experience' would it not be too late to interpose the illusory color-switching-while-moving scene between the conscious experience of spot 1 and the conscious experience of spot 2? ... [other experimenters] proposed that the intervening motion is produced retrospectively, built only after the second flash occurs, and 'projected backwards in time' ... But what does it mean that this experienced motion is 'projected backwards in time'?[33]

Presented in this way, the color-phi effect certainly seems puzzling, at least to philosopher Goodman. Dennett and Kinsbourne describe two standard cognitive ways of dealing with this effect. One, which they term 'Orwellian', is that we experience things in one way, but then revise our memories, much as Minitruth in Orwell's *Nineteen Eighty-Four* revised history. The color-phi effect thus becomes a post-hoc reinterpretation: two spots are experienced, but a smoothly moving, color-changing spot is reported. Dennett and Kinsbourne term the other standard approach 'Stalinesque', by analogy with Stalin's show trials, in which false evidence is created but reported accurately. In this view, what is reported is what was actually experienced, though what was experienced was not what (objectively) happened. Dennett and Kinsbourne dismiss both these accounts in favor of what they term a 'multiple-drafts' model: 'Our Multiple Drafts model agrees with Goodman that retrospectively the brain creates the content (the judgment) that there was intervening motion, and that this content is then available to govern activity and leave its mark on memory. But our model claims that the brain does not bother "constructing" any representations that go to the trouble of "filling in" the blanks.'[34] In the multiple-drafts model consciousness becomes a distributed construct, like 'The British Empire' (their analogy), which is not uniquely located in time or space.

Theoretical behaviorism has a much simpler way of looking at the color-phi effect. First, note that like all other psychological phenomena, the effect involves three conceptually separate domains:

Domain 1. The first is the domain of felt experience, the *phenomenological* domain. There is a certain quality (philosophers call this *quale*) associated with the color-phi experience. This is subjective and we can say nothing about it directly. From a scientific point of view, I cannot say whether 'green' looks the same to you as to me; I can only say whether or not you make the same judgments about colored objects as I do.[35] I can also know if you say the same things about color-phi-type stimuli as I do. Note that this is a behavioristic position, but it is not the version of behaviorism dismissed by Dennett and Kinsbourne, when they say 'One could, then, "make the problems disappear" by simply refusing to take introspective reports seriously.'[36] As we will see shortly, the question is not whether phenomenological reports should be ignored, but what to do with them.

Domain 2. The second domain is physiological, the real-time functioning of the brain. The color-phi experiment says nothing about the brain, but another experiment, which I will discuss in a moment, does include physiological data.

Domain 3. The third domain is the domain of behavioral data, 'intersubjectively verifiable' reports and judgments by experimental subjects. The reports of people in response to appropriate stimuli are the basis for everything objective we can know about color-phi.

I believe that much of the muddle in the various cognitive accounts arises first of all from confusion among these three domains. For example, Dennett and Kinsbourne write: 'Conscious experiences are real events occurring in the real time and space of the brain, and hence they are clockable and locatable within the appropriate limits of precision for real phenomena of their type.'[37] Well, no, not really. What can be clocked and located are *reports* of conscious experiences and *measurements* of physiological events. Conscious experiences are *Domain 1*, which has neither time nor space, but only ineffable *qualia*. The only evidence we have for these *qualia* (at least, for someone else's) is *Domain 3*. And we can try and correlate *Domain 3* data with *Domain 2* data and infer something about the brain correlates of reported experiences. But that's all. Despite Dennett and Kinsbourne's picturesque prose, their discussion leaves us in a muddle.

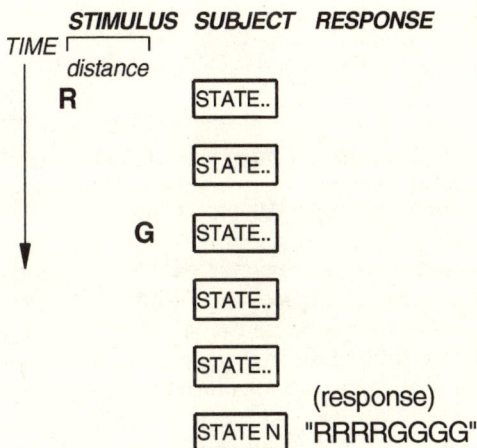

Color-phi Experiment

Fig. 5.1. Event-history in the color-phi experiment. A red spot (**R**) is briefly lit at time 0, a little later a green spot (**G**) is lit. After an additional short delay, the subject responds that he has seen a moving spot that changes color ('RRRRGGGG').

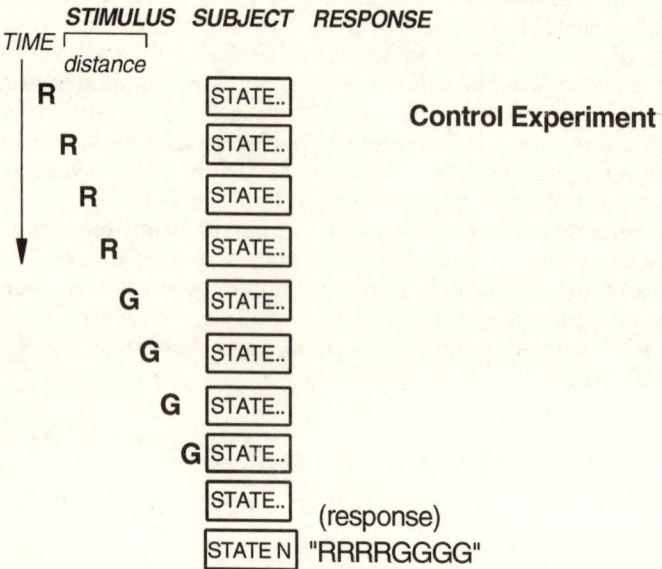

Fig. 5.2. Event history in a control experiment. A smoothly moving illuminated spot changes color mid-way from red to green. After a delay, the subject reports veridically ('RRRRGGGG').

All becomes much clearer once we look more closely at *Domain 3*: What did the subjects see? What did they say about it, and when did they say it? The real-time events in the color-phi experiment are illustrated in Fig. 5.1, which is a version of the general framework of Box 5.4 tailored to this experiment. Time goes from top to bottom in discrete steps.[38] At time 0 the red spot is lit and goes out; there is a delay; then the green spot is lit; there is another delay and then the subject reports what he has seen, namely a continuously moving red spot that changes to green half way through its travel: 'RRRRGGGG.' Everything in the diagram is *Domain 3*,[39] except the subject's response 'RRRRGGGG'. What does this response mean? This seems to be the heart of the puzzle, but the unknowable *quale* here is scientifically irrelevant. What it can tell us is something about other, 'control' experiments that might give the *same* quale. Fig.

104

5.2 shows one such control experiment. In this experiment, a single spot really is moving and changing color at the midpoint: RRRRGGGG, and the subject's report is appropriately 'RRRRGGGG.' The similarity between the responses to the objectively moving stimulus and to the color-phi stimulus is what the statement 'the color-phi stimulus looks like a continuously moving spot that changes color' means. The point is that *we* (i.e. an external observer) cannot judge the subject's quale, but we *can* judge if his response is the same or different on two occasions. And as for the subject, he can also judge whether one thing looks like another or not. These same-different judgments are all that is required for a scientific account.

The comparison between these two experiments suggests an answerable scientific problem, namely: 'What kinds of process give the same output to the two different histories illustrated in the two figures?' More generally, what characterizes the class of histories that give the response 'RRRRGGGG'? The answer will be some kind of well-defined process, which can be simulated on a computer or built in to a microchip. One can even get a glimpse of the appropriate process. It will be one in which the representations of temporally adjacent events tend to inhibit one another, so that 'end' events are more salient than events in the middle of a series. Thus, the sequence RRRRGGGG might be registered as something like RRRRGGGG – which might well resemble the registered color-phi sequence R ... G, so that both will give rise to the same response. No doubt there are many other theoretical possibilities.[40]

Note that no problem is posed by the fact that processed sequence RRRRGGGG is different from the input sequence RRRRGGGG. The point is how a given representation is *interpreted* by the brain, not whether it resembles in some specific way the property of the external world that produced it. The 'copy theory' of perception is generally false.

Dennett and Kinsbourne also discuss conscious effects of electrical brain stimulation that have elicited almost mystical responses from susceptible commentators. In a provocative series of experiments, Benjamin Libet has studied the relation between recorded and applied brain electrical events and reports of consciousness. For example, in one experiment Libet studied the tingling sensation that can be produced by a brief electrical pulse to the hand (the *left* hand, say). He found that a similar sensation could be produced by stimulating the subject's cortex (say the *left* cortex, so that the sensation is referred to the *right* hand). Libet has reported instances in which the subject's left cortex (sensation in *right* hand) was stimulated *before* his *left* hand, yet the subject's reported sensations in the reverse order: first *left* hand, then *right*. Libet himself views these results as a challenge to materialism, and respected knights of science and philosophy Sir John Eccles and Sir Karl Popper seem to agree.[41]

It's hard to see why these results amaze. The subject's report in every case comes after the stimulating events have ceased – no time-reversal has occurred. An electrical stimulus to the cortex that is quite different from any naturally generated brain event might well take longer to interpret than a stimulus applied to sensory end-organs expressly evolved to receive stimuli. Hence, it should not surprise that the brain-induced sensation is reported as occurring after the peripherally produced one. The reversal of temporal order is puzzling only if we have some idea that consciousness is a sort of driving force, rather than a property of our system for self-report.

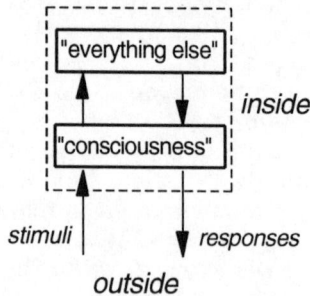

Fig. 5.3. Schematic diagram for a suggested relation between two brain subsystems: the part devoted to 'consciousness', and 'everything else'. Consciousness communicates with the outside world and also receives input from everything else (i.e. the unconscious systems of the brain). Each step – from outside world to consciousness, from consciousness to everything else, and back, and the response – takes some time. In such a system, brain signals directly from everything else may precede the response of recognition from consciousness.

5. Mind and Mechanism: Behaviorism Today

But Libet is not through. In another experiment puzzling to some he asked subjects to make 'spontaneous' decisions to move one hand while looking at a clock and noting the precise time they 'formed the intention' to move. Libet recorded the movement, the judged time of the intention, and the time of the pre-intentional 'readiness potentials' on the surface of the subjects' scalps. He found that times subjects reported for the genesis of their intentions lagged behind the readiness potentials by almost half a second. This seems to rule out a real 'executive' role for consciousness.

This result is interesting, but not in any way paradoxical – unless one has a rather naive view of consciousness as a 'first cause' of action. The control scheme illustrated in Fig. 5.3, for example, is perfectly consistent with Libet's result. The idea is that the 'consciousness' functional subsystem receives input from the outside world and passes on instructions to 'everything else' to produce the desired behavior according to the required 'spontaneous' rule. Libet's 'readiness potentials' come from everything else, not from 'consciousness'. In turn, whenever 'everything else', following the rule as instructed, initiates an action, it reports its behavior to 'consciousness'. Each of these steps takes some time. Thus, the action of 'everything else', reflected immediately in its readiness potential, occurs before 'consciousness' has time to process the incoming report that an action is imminent and to note the real time coming in on the 'stimulus' line. No doubt there are many other functional arrangements that can duplicate the time delays that Libet found.

Dissociations of the sort just described can be observed without EEG paraphernalia. If you have ever participated in a quiz under time pressure you know that very often you *know that you know* the answer to a question quite some time before the answer itself arrives in consciousness. Sometimes, of course, the delay is very long indeed. In the so-called 'tip-of-the-tongue' phenomenon, for example, you may have the 'feeling of knowing' days before the answer pops into consciousness. If something corresponding to Libet's readiness potential could be measured, perhaps it would occur more or less contemporaneously with the 'feeling of knowing' and thus some time before the actual answer becomes available. According to the scheme illustrated in Fig. 5.3, the feeling of knowing is transmitted to consciousness from 'everything else' in advance of the actual information desired –

and in response to a 'request' for the information from consciousness.

The muddled cognitive view of consciousness grows out of a conflation of the subjective (*Domain 1*) and objective (*Domains 2 and 3*) levels. (We saw a similar conflation of subjective and objective in Skinner's analysis of freedom and responsibility in Chapter 4). This conflation has led to needless puzzles about the issues raised by experiments like these. Moreover, the naive and dismissive view of behaviorism shared, in a fashionable 'cognitive correctness', by much of the psychological community, has prevented serious consideration of the kinds of arguments I have just offered.[42] The behaviorists themselves are partly to blame, of course, as I have pointed out in the preceding chapters. Nevertheless, the lack of a behavioristic perspective on these problems has allowed views that often verge on the mystical to gain a respectful audience.

*

Behaviorism was once the dominant movement in American psychology. It was eclipsed by the 'cognitive revolution' in the late 1970s. Two things seem to have favored the cognitive movement: First, the digital computer, which for the first time allowed mentalistic ideas to be simulated and overcame behavioristic criticisms that cognitive theories were inexact and anecdotal. Secondly, the takeover of behaviorism by Skinnerian radical behaviorism with its strong bias against formal theory and its belief that psychology is nothing but the collection of orderly experimental data. Radical behaviorism blocked theoretical advances within behaviorism so that *connectionism*, the next evolutionary step in the associationistic tradition of the early behaviorists, was forced to find a home in cognitive, rather than behavioristic, psychology.

In recent years, cognitivism has come under increasing attack. The computer metaphor has been criticized as fundamentally inadequate, and workers on behavior-based artificial intelligence have suggested that the cognitive-science approach through *representation* has failed to achieve real intelligence. Lower-level, nonsymbolic tasks, they argue, are more fundamental to biological intelligence, evolved earlier, and are more difficult to recreate by artificial methods. At the same time, a new theoretical behaviorism is emerging that shares the behavior-based-AI emphasis on intelligent behavior as the outcome of interactions among independent, unintelligent agents. Theoretical behaviorism can deal with mentalistic problems like 'consciousness' without either ignoring them, obscuring the distinction between what is inside vs. what is outside the organism (like radical behaviorism), or confusing what is felt with what can be measured (like some recent cognitive discussions). Theoretical behaviorism promises to provide theoretical links between behavior and the brain that rest on real understanding, rather than on mentalistic presumptions about how brain-behavior relations 'must' be arranged.

Notes

Chapter 1

1. Fans of dichotomies like this should consult R.I. Watson's (1971) list of eighteen, which reduces psychology to something resembling diced pork: 'Prescriptions as operative in the history of psychology', *Journal of the History of the Behavioral Sciences* **7**, 311-22.

2. Amsel, A. (1989) *Behaviorism, neobehaviorism and cognitivism in learning theory*. Hillsdale: Erlbaum, p. 1.

3. Ridley, M. (1992) *Nature* **359**, 280.

4. Watson, J.B. (1913) 'Psychology as the behaviorist views it', *Psychological Review* **20**, 158-77.

5. Meyer, M. (1921) *The psychology of the other one: an introductory textbook of psychology*. Columbia: Missouri Book.

6. 'Psychology as the behaviorist views it', op. cit., p. 158.

7. Ziman, J. (1968) *Public knowledge: the social dimension of science*. Cambridge University Press.

8. Pippard, B. (1992) *Nature* **357**, 29.

9. The early history of animal psychology is engagingly described in Boakes, R. (1984) *From Darwin to behaviourism: psychology and the minds of animals*. Cambridge University Press.

10. Thorndike, E.L. (1898) 'Animal intelligence: An experimental study of the associative processes in animals', *Psychological Review Monographs, Suppl. 2* [8]. The law of effect was not original with Thorndike. Alexander Bain had come to a very similar conclusion more than forty years earlier; but Thorndike's version is the one in all the textbooks.

11. Hull, C.L. (1943) *The principles of behavior*. New York: Appleton-Century.

12. Charles S. Sherrington (1856-1952) was an English physiologist whose book, *The integrative action of the nervous system* (Silliman Lectures) (New Haven: Yale University Press, 1906), summarized most of what was then known about the reflex and exterted a strong influence on the evolution of American psychology, especially behaviorism.

13. Bower, G.H. & Hilgard, E.R. (1981) *Theories of learning* (5th ed.). Englewood Cliffs: Prentice-Hall.

14. See, for example, the survey volumes edited by Luce, R.D., Bush, R.R. & Galanter, E. (eds.) (1963) *Handbook of mathematical psychology* (3 vols.). New York: Wiley.

15. Rescorla, R.A. & Wagner, A.R. (1972) 'A theory of Pavlovian conditioning: variations in the effectiveness of reinforcement and non-reinforcement' in Black, A. & Prokasy, W.F. (eds.) *Classical conditioning: II. Current research and theory*. New York: Appleton- Century-Crofts.

16. Hull, C.L., Hovland, C.I., Ross, R.T., Hall, M., Perkins, D.T. & Fitch, F.G. (1940) *Mathematico-deductive theory of rote learning*. New York: McGraw-Hill.

17. An 'error' is defined as a wrong choice from the point of view of getting from start box to goal in the maze.

18. Blodgett, H.C. (1929) 'The effect of the introduction of reward upon the maze performance of rats', *University of California Publications in Psychology* 4, 113-34. Tolman, E.C. & Honzik, C.H. (1930) 'Introduction and removal of reward and maze performance in rats', *University of California Publications in Psychology* 4, 257-75. See also Tolman, E.C. (1932) *Purposive behavior in animals and men*. New York: Century.

19. Tolman, E.C. & Honzik, C.H. (1930) ' "Insight" in rats', *University of California Publications in Psychology* 4, 215-32.

20. 'Behaviorism is founded upon natural science; structural psychology is based upon a crude dualism, the roots of which extend far back into theological mysticism' (Watson, J.B., *Psychology from the standpoint of a behaviorist*. Philadelphia: Lippincott. 3rd edition, 1929, p. viii).

21. See, for example, Roitblat, H.L., Bever, T.G. & Terrace, H.S. (eds.) (1984) *Animal cognition*. Hillsdale: Erlbaum.

22. After the wonderful doctor in Hugh Lofting's books for children who could understand the speech of animals.

Chapter 2

1. Contemporary views of Skinner and Skinnerianism by several authors were recently collected in 'Reflections on B.F. Skinner and Psychology', *American Psychologist* 47 (whole issue), 1992. Many of these papers attempt to combat misrepresentations of Skinner.

2. Skinner, B.F. (1950/1961) 'Are theories of learning necessary?' reprinted in Skinner, B.F. (1961) *Cumulative record*, 2nd ed. New York: Appleton-Century-Crofts, p. 39.

3. Skinner's life is rather bleakly recounted in his three-volume autobiography *Particulars of my life* (1976), *The shaping of a behaviorist* (1979), and *A matter of consequences* (1983) New York: Alfred Knopf.

4. Skinner, B.F. (1956/1961) 'A case history in scientific method', reprinted in *Cumulative record*, op. cit., pp. 78-9.

5. Skinner's serendipitous development of the Skinner box, and his informal approach to science generally are described in *A case history in scientific method* and other papers in *Cumulative record*. His dissertation research and the associated theoretical system are described in his most important technical book *The behavior of organisms*. New York: Appleton-Century-Crofts (1938).

6. For a summary of Mowrer's ideas see Mowrer, O.H. (1960) *Learning theory and behavior.* New York: Wiley. See also Dollard, J. & Miller, N.E. (1950) *Personality and psychotherapy.* New York: McGraw-Hill. See also E.C. Tolman (1942) *Drives toward war.* New York: Appleton-Century.

7. In an interview near the end of his life Skinner advised a young psychologist 'Never argue' (A. Machado, pers. comm.) It was a principle he followed with almost no exceptions. Avoidance of debate may be good advice for the would-be hostess ('If you can't say something good, say nothing at all'). It is not usually thought to be a good way of rooting out error.

8. The responding probably was not yet stable, because typical behavior for animals long trained on a fixed-interval schedule is not a steady rate, but a pause after each food delivery followed by responding at an accelerating rate until the next food delivery (see Fig. 2.2).

9. Ferster, C.B. & Skinner, B.F. (1957) *Schedules of reinforcement.* New York: Appleton-Century-Crofts.

10. Sidman, M. (1960) *The tactics of scientific research.* New York: Basic Books.

11. For discussions of the problem of reversibility see Davis, D.G.S., Staddon, J.E.R., Machado, A. & Palmer, R.G. (1993) 'The process of recurrent choice', *Psychological Review* **100**, 320-41, and Staddon, J.E.R. 'The conventional wisdom of behavior analysis', *Journal of the Experimental Analysis of Behavior* (1993, in press).

12. Herrnstein, R.J. (1961) 'Relative and absolute strength of response as a function of frequency of reinforcement', *Journal of the Experimental Analysis of Behavior* **4**, 267-72.

13. New York: Knopf, 1971.

14. Keller, F.S. & Schoenfeld, W.N. (1950) *Principles of psychology.* New York: Appleton-Century-Crofts.

15. Skinner, B.F. (1950) 'Are theories of learning necessary?', *Psychological Review* **57**, 193-216. Reprinted in *Cumulative record* (1961), op. cit., p. 69. Notice that this definition excludes any attention to the *process* that underlies learning.

16. Smith, L.D. (1986) *Behaviorism and logical positivism.* Stanford University Press, p. 272.

17. Skinner, B.F. (1969) *Contingencies of reinforcement: a theoretical analysis.* New York: Appleton-Century-Crofts.

18. The quote is from Skinner's undergraduate textbook: Skinner, B.F. (1953) *Science and human behavior.* New York: Macmillan, p. 64.

19. It is unfortunate that the same word, *contingency*, is used in these two rather different senses: to mean either causal dependence (Skinner's sense), or a special kind of predictiveness (the usage common in non-Skinnerian learning psychology). I will try to make clear when I use the word just which sense is intended.

20. The seminal paper here is Rescorla, R.A. (1967) 'Pavlovian conditioning and its proper control procedures', *Psychological Review* **74**, 71-80.

21. Skinner changed the definition of the *response* away from either a physical movement or set of physical movements – or some kind of cognitively defined act - to that class of physical movements that are effective in producing a given reinforcer. The discriminative stimulus was by implication defined in a similar way (see Staddon, J.E.R. (1967) 'Asymptotic behavior: the concept of the operant', *Psychological Review* **74**, 377-91.)

22. Reynolds, G.S. (1961) 'Behavioral contrast', *Journal of the Experimental Analysis of Behavior* **4**, 57-71.

23. Guttman, N. & Kalish, H.I. (1956) 'Discriminability and stimulus generalization', *Journal of Experimental Psychology* **51**, 79-88.

24. Simon, H.A. (1987) 'Rational decision-making in business organizations' in Green, L. & Kagel, J.H. (eds.) *Advances in behavioral economics,* vol. 1. Norwood, NJ: Ablex, pp. 18-47. Reprint of 1978 Nobel address, p. 19.

25. Wynne, C.D.L. & Staddon, J.E.R. (1988) 'Typical delay determines waiting time on periodic-food schedules: static and dynamic tests', *Journal of the Experimental Analysis of Behavior* **50**, 197-210.

26. See, for example, Mazur, J.E. (1981) 'Optimization theory fails to predict performance of pigeons in a two-response situation', *Science* **214**, 823-5, and Staddon, J.E.R. & Hinson, J.M. (1983) 'Optimization: a result or a mechanism?', *Science* **221**, 976-7.

27. The new movement that calls itself socio-economics, for example, seeks to explore the psychological and social determinants of economic behavior. See the collection of papers edited by Amitai Etzioni (1991) *Socio-economics: toward a new synthesis.* Armonk, NY: M.E. Sharpe Inc.

28. A number of papers discussing the relevance of economic ideas to psychological and biological problems is collected in Staddon, J.E.R. (ed.) (1980). *Limits to action: the allocation of individual behavior.* New York: Academic Press. The economic approach to psychological problems is also discussed in McKenzie, R.B. & Tullock, G. (1981) *The new world of economics: exploration into the human experience.* Homewood, IL: Richard Irwin (3rd ed.). See also the series *Advances in behavioral economics,* edited by L. Green and J. Kagel (Norwood, NJ: Ablex) and Gary Becker (1976) *The economic approach to human behavior.* University of Chicago Press. F.A. Hayek and others in the Austrian school anticipated some of these ideas; see, for example, Mises, L. von (1949) *Human action.* New Haven: Yale University Press.

29. Other than through the idea of 'conditioned reinforcement', but this notion obviously does not apply to things like narcotics. And as we have seen, in the animal laboratory conditioned reinforcement is almost invariably a rather weak effect that disappears rapidly once the sustaining primary reinforcement (such as food) is withdrawn.

Chapter 3

1. Skinner, B.F. (1948) ' "Superstition" in the pigeon', *Journal of Experimental Psychology* **38**, 168-72. Reprinted in *Cumulative record*, op. cit.

2. E.g. in the text by Henton, W.W. & Iversen, I.H. (1978) *Classical conditioning and operant conditioning*. New York: Springer-Verlag.

3. ' "Superstition" in the pigeon', op. cit., p. 171.

4. Brown, P.L. & Jenkins, H.M. (1968) 'Auto-shaping of the pigeon's key peck', *Journal of the Experimental Analysis of Behavior* **11**, 1-8. Williams, D.R. & Williams, H. (1969) 'Auto-maintenance in the pigeon: sustained pecking despite contingent nonreinforcement', *Journal of the Experimental Analysis of Behavior* **12**, 511-20.

5. Staddon, J.E.R. & Simmelhag, V. (1971). 'The "superstition" experiment: a re-examination of its implications for the principles of adaptive behavior', *Psychological Review* **78**, 3-43.

6. Staddon, J.E.R. & Zhang, Y. (1991) 'On the assignment-of-credit problem in operant learning' in Commons, M.L., Grossberg, S. & Staddon J.E.R. (eds.) *Neural networks of conditioning and action, the XIIth Harvard Symposium*. Hillsdale, NJ: Erlbaum Associates, pp. 279-93. 'Assignment of credit' is a technical term from artificial intelligence which refers to a problem for all adaptive systems: deciding which act (or which property of their internal state) is responsible for good or bad things that have occurred. Operant conditioning involves assignment of credit in the sense that the organism always has to decide which action was responsible for the reward.

7. A variety of failures of the operant-conditioning method in species ranging from raccoons to chickens was described in an important paper by two erstwhile collaborators of Skinner's, Marion and Keller Breland: Breland, K. & Breland, M. (1960) 'The misbehavior of organisms', *American Psychologist* **16**, 661-4. The Brelands coined the term 'instinctive drift' for a curious effect whereby reinforcement for one behavior ends up strengthening another, 'instinctive' behavior.

8. Killeen, P.R. (1978) 'Superstition: a matter of bias, not detectability', *Science* **199**, 88-90.

9. See for example critical theorist Barbara Herrnstein Smith (1988) *Contingencies of value: alternative perspectives for critical theory*. Cambridge: Harvard University Press, which describes a basically Skinnerian philosophy she terms 'relativism'. Relativism seems to deny (it is hard to be sure) the existence of objective truth, even in principle: '[relativism is] any more or less extensively theorized questioning – analysis, problematizing, critique – of the key elements of objectivist thought and its attendant axiological machinery' (p. 151). This is not the first time that an influential psychological approach has been taken up by the literati. The decline of psychoanalysis as a scientific discipline coincided with the appropriation of psychoanalytic ideas into literary criticism. Freud's 'psychoanalytic method' was neither analytic nor a (scientific) method in anything but a metaphorical sense, of course – Skinner's ideas are much better grounded in experiment than were Freud's. What (we may nevertheless wonder) portends the take-up of Skinner's ideas by the literary community?

10. Skinner, B.F. (1966) *Science* **153**, 1205-13. See also Skinner, B.F. (1981) 'Selection by consequences', *Science* **213**, 501-4.

11. E.g. Baldwin, J.M. (1902) *Development and evolution*. New York: Macmillan. Hull's views are discussed in Amsel, A. & Rashotte, M.E. (eds.) (1984) *Mechanisms of adaptive behavior: Clark L. Hull's theoretical papers, with commentary*. New York: Columbia Press.

12. Ashby, W.R. (1952) *Design for a brain*. London: Chapman & Hall: 'The work ... develops a theory of the "natural selection" of behaviour-patterns' (p. vi); Campbell, D.T. (1956) 'Adaptive behavior from random response', *Behavioral Science* **1**, 105-10. Popper, K.R. (1972) *Objective knowledge: an evolutionary approach*. Oxford: Clarendon Press. See also Pringle, J.W.S. (1951) 'On the parallel between learning and evolution', *Behaviour* **3**, 174-215. For a recent attempt to relate the Darwinian metaphor for operant behavior to work on neural networks see Palmer, D.C. & Donahoe, J.W. (1992) 'Essentialism and selectionism in cognitive science and behavior analysis', *American Psychologist* **47**, 1344-58. See also Edelman, G.M. (1987) *Neural Darwinism*. New York: Basic Books.

13. The pejorative term is from Stephen Jay Gould, who has used it in his many critiques of adaptationist arguments.

14. *Science and human behavior*, op. cit., p. 91.

15. Staddon & Simmelhag, op. cit., p. 31.

16. E.g. Machado, A. (1992) 'Behavioral variability and frequency-dependent selection', *Journal of the Experimental Analysis of Behavior* **58**, 241-63.

17. Staddon, J.E.R. (1975) 'A note on the evolutionary significance of supernormal stimuli', *American Naturalist* **109**, 541-5.

18. Some of these issues as they relate to operant psychology are discussed in Staddon, J.E.R. (1983) *Adaptive behavior and learning*. New York: Cambridge University Press, pp. xiii, 1-555; Staddon (1991) 'Selective choice: a commentary on Herrnstein (1990)', *American Psychologist* **46**, 793-7, and references therein.

19. Actually, Darwinian fitness depends on *reproduction*, not just survival, but Skinner's phrase is perhaps more vivid.

20. Campbell, D.T. (1975) 'On the conflicts between biological and social evolution and between psychology and moral tradition', *American Psychologist* **30**, 1103-26 at p. 1103.

21. See for example, the Dahlem Conference report edited by Stent, G. (1980) *Morality as a biological phenomenon*. University of California Press, and the recent collection of papers edited by Barkow, J.H., Cosmides, L. & Tooby, J. (1992) *The adapted mind: evolutionary psychology and the generation of culture*. New York: Oxford University Press.

Chapter 4

1. Skinner, B.F. (1976) *About behaviorism*. New York: Vintage Books, p. 3.

2. New York: Knopf, 1971. See also Skinner's utopian novel *Walden two* (New York: Macmillan, 1948), which discusses many of the same issues.

3. Stephen Stich has also made this point in Catania, A.C. & Harnad, S. (1988) *The selection of behavior. The operant behaviorism of B.F. Skinner: comments and consequences*. Cambridge University Press, p. 361.

4. There are many versions of evolutionary epistemology. I am giving an eclectic view that draws on the works of many writers. For a historical survey of epistemology in general see Bertrand Russell's (1946) *History of Western philosophy*. London: Allen & Unwin. Recent discussions of evolutionary epistemology are Hull, D.L. (1988) *Science as a process*. Chicago: University of Chicago Press, and Radnitzky, G. & Bartley, W.W. (eds) (1987) *Evolutionary epistemology, rationality, and the sociology of knowledge*. Illinois: Open Court.

5. Karl Popper (1962), paraphrasing Bertrand Russell, in *Conjectures and refutations: the growth of scientific knowledge*. New York: Basic Books, pp. 4-5.

6. Skinner, B.F. (1945/1961) 'The operational analysis of psychological terms' in *Cumulative record*, op. cit., p. 282.

7. Some of my criticisms of *Beyond freedom and dignity*, together with many others, are to be found in a long review by Noam Chomsky ('Psychology and ideology', *Cognition* **1**, 11-46, 1972.) This forceful critique, slightly marred by a self-satisfied ideology different from, but at least as sure of itself as Skinner's own less obvious one, is a continuation of Chomsky's earlier attack on Skinner's 1958 book *Verbal behavior* (New York: Appleton-Century-Crofts): Chomsky, N. (1959) 'A review of B.F. Skinner's *Verbal behavior*', *Language* **35**, 26-58. Unfortunately, these attacks served only to isolate Skinnerians from the mainstream of psychology. Many of Chomsky's criticisms are well founded – most non-Skinnerians assume that all are.

But Chomsky was largely dismissed by Skinnerians because he failed to understand Skinner's main, pragmatic objective. Much of Chomsky's critique of Skinner's view of language, for example, is irrelevant because Chomsky's criticisms are from the point of view of someone interested in the structural – syntactic – properties of language, whereas Skinner was interested only in its functional properties: how language evolved and is used, rather than what it is.

8. Op. cit., p. 96.

9. Op. cit., p. 17.

10. There is a lengthy legal literature on the improper use of rewards (e.g. rewarding prisoners for undergoing treatments they would not willingly submit to if not incarcerated), but this example does not fall under that head. See Posner, R.A. (1990) *The problems of jurisprudence*, Harvard University Press, for a relatively sophisticated account of the relations between philosophy, psychology and jurisprudence.

11. There is no place in Skinner's philosophy for *feelings* of course, although he uses the word freely in *Beyond freedom and dignity*. But this statement could be restated in a behavioristically acceptable form ('appropriate verbal behavior' and the like) if necessary.

12. Although he disclaims any such intention in the beginning of *Beyond freedom and dignity*: 'The importance of the literature of freedom can scarcely be questioned ... [it] has made an essential contribution to the elimination of many aversive practices in government, religion, education, family life, and the production of goods' (p. 29). Nevertheless, the overwhelming thrust of the book is to disparage. The next paragraph gets to Skinner's main point: 'Some traditional theories could conceivably be said to define freedom as the absence of aversive control, but the emphasis has been on how that condition *feels*.' 'Freedom' is a feeling, of course, and when his guard is down Skinner himself says things like individuals should 'enjoy the greatest sense of freedom' and the like.

13. The cost of errors – punishing innocent people – must also be included, of course. But the effectiveness of punishment depends on this number being as small as possible – this is the issue of *contingency* discussed in Chapter 2. Crime must predict punishment, in the sense I described, if it is to be an effective deterrent. Unjust punishment also entails many other problems, so every consideration points to the importance of justice. There remains the problem of how 'suffering' might be measured. There are behavioral methods that can shed some light on this question, which must be confronted by any philosophy of social welfare, but I have no space to deal with them here.

14. Ibid., pp. 57-8.

15. An example of such a schedule is *shock postponement*. The rat subject receives brief electric shocks every 20 seconds (say). But if he presses a lever, the next shock is postponed for 20 seconds. By pressing the lever more often than every 20 seconds, the rat can avoid shock completely. Such a schedule is sometimes difficult to learn, but once learned the behavior can persist indefinitely, even if the shock generator is turned off. Laboratory experiments on avoidance schedules are described in chapters by Morse and Kelleher, and Hineline in Honig, W.K. & Staddon, J.E.R. (eds.) (1977) *Handbook of operant behavior.* New York: Prentice-Hall.

16. Organized rebellions, like the French and Russian revolutions and the current turmoil in South Africa, are usually associated with periods when aversive contingencies are relaxed rather than with their high points. But Skinner would probably have argued that without the contingencies, the rebellions need never have occurred.

17. It may well be that ratio schedules have 'aversive aspects'. With small rewards, or very large ratios, animals show 'strain' – increasing reluctance to respond. The theoretical problem is to define ahead of time the conditions under which a schedule of positive reinforcement is also aversive. Skinner's approach provides no answer to this question other than to actually try the schedule in question.

18. Darwin, C. (1872/1951) *The origin of species*, Oxford University Press, a reprint of the 1872 edition, p. 217, my emphasis.

19. See, for example, Dinsmoor, J.A. (1992) 'Setting the record straight: the social views of B.F. Skinner' in *Reflections on B.F. Skinner and psychology*, op. cit.

20. Psychologists are always the first to urge attention to 'root causes' of crime – poverty, family structure, racism, almost anything but the absence of consistent discipline in the home, at school, and from law enforcement – whenever there is a large-scale breakdown of civil order.

21. W.V.O. Quine, quoted in Judge Richard Posner's book *The problems of jurisprudence*, op. cit., p. 176.

22. *Beyond freedom and dignity*, op. cit., pp. 99, 102.

23. See, for example, Moore, G.E. (1903) *Principia ethica.* Cambridge University Press. Skinner was much influenced by Bertrand Russell, Moore and the Cambridge School of philosophy.

24. *Beyond freedom and dignity*, op. cit., p. 104.

25. Interestingly a very similar argument has been made in economics. Successful firms, it is argued, are not necessarily smarter or better at computing marginal utilities than unsuccessful; they may just have begun with a 'corporate culture' that happens to be more successful under the prevailing conditions. See, for example, Sydney Winter (1964) 'Economic natural selection and the theory of the firm', *Yale Economic Essays* **4**, 225-72.

26. In the Darwinian sense, i.e. more likely to persist.

27. There is of course a vast literature on the problem of whether or not values can be derived through reason from facts. The philosophical consensus seems to be that 'the Enlightenment project', as this endeavor has been termed, is, and must be, a failure. See, for example, MacIntyre, A. (1981) *After virtue* (London: Duckworth) for a contemporary survey.

28. *About behaviorism*, op. cit., pp. 242-3.

29. Op. cit., pp. 30-1.

30. See my comment on Skinner's *Behaviorism at fifty* and Skinner's response, reprinted in *The selection of behavior*, op. cit., pp. 360-1.

31. *About behaviorism*, op. cit., p. 91.

32. Evidence is not totally lacking, however. Roger Shepard has done a famous series of experiments in which subjects are asked to identify an object as the same or different from a target object. On each trial either the target object, or its mirror image are presented. Shepard found that the time taken to respond correctly is proportional to the number of degrees the test object must be rotated to bring it into registry with the target object – suggesting that subjects 'rotate a mental image' in their heads. See Shepard, R.N. & Metzler, J. (1971) 'Mental rotation of three-dimensional objects', *Science* 171, 701-3.

33. I am excluding physiological causes, of course. Physiological processes of memory bridge the temporal gap between events in an individual's past history and their effects as present behavior.

34. This ideology is not the one criticized by Chomsky in his polemical review, *Psychology and ideology*, op. cit. Chomsky objects to Skinner's assumption that human behavior will turn out to be perfectly determined by environment and heredity. I object to Skinner's disingenuous dismissal of punishment. It is worth noting that determinism is not contrary to free will and the assumption of determinism is essential to the scientific study of behavior. Chomsky's ill-conceived objections to determinism were unfortunately as influential as Skinner's equally mistaken opposition between free-will and determinism.

35. *Science and human behavior*, op. cit., pp. 12-13.

Chapter 5

1. Wispé, L.G. & Thompson, J.N. (1976) 'The war between the words: biological versus social evolution and some related issues', *American Psychologist* 31, 341-7 at p. 346.

2. James, W. (1890) *Principles of psychology*. New York: Holt. George A. Miller used this sentence of James's to announce the first salvo of the mentalistic counter-revolution in his 1962 book *Psychology: the science of mental life*. Harper & Row.

3. Johnson-Laird, P.N. (1988) *The computer and the mind*. Harvard University Press, pp. 17-18.

4. Newell, A., Shaw, J.C. & Simon, H.A. (1957) 'Empirical explorations of the logic theory machine: a case study in heuristic', *Proceedings of the Western Joint Computer Conference*, Institute of Radio Engineers

(February), pp. 218-30, reprinted in Feigenbaum, E.A. & Feldman, J. (eds.) (1963) *Computers and thought*. New York: McGraw-Hill, pp. 109-33. For some of the more confident prophecies from the new cognitive psychology see the collection of papers in Simon, H.A. (1979) *Models of thought*. New Haven: Yale University Press.

5. The terminology in this area is confusing. *Cognitive psychology* is the movement I have been describing; cognitive science is a slightly broader term that also includes workers in artificial intelligence, linguistics and other ancillary disciplines who share an interest in human thought.

6. This is a very widely accepted view in cognition; see, for example, Johnson-Laird, *The computer and the mind*, op. cit.; Pylyshyn, Z. (1984) *Computation and cognition: toward a foundation for cognitive science*. Bradford Books, MIT Press; Feigenbaum, E. & Feldman, J. (eds.) (1963) *Computers and thought*, New York: McGraw-Hill. The founding genius for this view was Alan Turing ('Computing machinery and intelligence', *Mind* **59**, 433-60, 1950). Turing proposed as a test for 'thought' a comparison between the responses to typed questions of a human being and an appropriately programmed computer. If an observer cannot tell from the responses whether the agent is a man or a machine, then 'thought' should be conceded to the machine as well as to the man. Passing the 'Turing test' is the avowed objective of modern cognitive science. Searle objects that even if the test is passed, the successful program need not be accepted as a valid theory of the human mind.

7. Searle, J. (1992) *The rediscovery of the mind*. Bradford Books, MIT Press, pp. 201-2. See also Dreyfus, H.L. (1972) *What computers can't do*, New York: Harper and Row, and Penrose, R. (1989) *The emperor's new mind*, Oxford University Press, for other influential attacks on 'strong AI'.

8. Op. cit., p. 214.

9. E.g. in Chomsky, N. (1964) *Current issues in linguistic theory*. The Hague: Mouton.

10. *The rediscovery of the mind*, op. cit., p. 247.

11. Brooks, R.A. (1991) 'Intelligence without representation', *Artificial Intelligence* **47**, 139-59 at p. 140.

12. Brooks, R.A., op. cit., p. 141.

13. Maes, P. (1992) 'Behavior-based artifical intelligence', *From animals to animats 2. Proceedings of the Second International Conference on the Simulation of Adaptive Behavior*. Cambridge: MIT Press, pp. 2-10.

14. These objections to representation may remind you of John Watson's objections to structuralism (see Chapter 1, n. 20.)

15. Books on neural nets have proliferated mightily in recent years. The now-classical source in psychology is McClelland, J. L., Rumelhart, D.E. & the PDP Research Group (1986) *Parallel distributed processing: explorations in the microstructure of cognition*, Vols 1 & 2. MIT Press. See also Grossberg, S. (1987) *The adapted brain*, Vols. I and II,

Amsterdam: North-Holland, and Hertz, J.A., Krogh, A. & Palmer, R.G. (1989) *Neural computation*, Reading, MA: Addison-Wesley. A physiologically oriented text is Churchland, P.S. & Sejnowski, T.J. (1992) *The computational brain*. MIT Press.

16. The most persistent and comprehensive effort was made by mathematician Stephen Grossberg. In a series of papers beginning in the 1960s he attempted to explain all the standard phenomena of animal learning in terms of formal neural networks. Unfortunately, his papers were for the most part long and difficult and his intended audience inadequately trained, and emotionally unprepared, to absorb them. His work had little influence on behaviorist thinking, but was eventually recognized by the formation of the new field of neural network theory of which he has become one of the leaders. For examples of Grossberg's work see *The adaptive brain*, op. cit. and *Studies of mind and brain*. Dordrecht, Holland: D. Reidel, 1982. Another early voice out of the behavioristic mainstream was Air Force researcher Harry Klopf. For a summary of some of this work, see his book *The hedonistic neuron: a theory of memory, learning and intelligence*. New York: Hemisphere, 1982. The idea of neural nets was introduced to psychology some years before all these efforts, by Donald Hebb in *The organization of behavior: a neurophysiological theory*, New York: John Wiley, 1949; but Hebb's ideas were very informal, couched in strictly physiological terms (rather than in terms of associations), and few unequivocal predictions about behavior could be derived from them. His idea about how connections between neurons are strengthened by experience lives on in neural-network theory, however. See Milner, P.M. (1992) 'The mind and Donald O. Hebb', *Scientific American* (January) 124-9.

17. See, for example, Pinker, S. & Mehler, J. (eds.) (1988) *Connections and symbols*. MIT Press.

18. Rachlin, H. (1992) 'Teleological behaviorism', *American Psychologist* **47**, 1371-1382, p. 1377.

19. Op. cit., p. 1372.

20. Rachlin, H (1992), op. cit. See also Rachlin's *Introduction to modern behaviorism* (3rd ed.) New York: Freeman, 1991.

21. *Science and human behavior*, op. cit., p. 279.

22. Rachlin (1992) op. cit., p. 1375.

23. Ainslie, G. (1992) *Picoeconomics*. Cambridge University Press, p. xii.

24. *Society of mind*. New York: Simon & Schuster, 1986.

25. See Staddon, 'The conventional wisdom of behavior analysis' and Davis et al., 'The process of recurrent choice', op. cit., ch. 1 n. 11. For earlier advocates of this approach see Minsky, M. (1969) *Computation: finite and infinite machines*, MIT Press, and Staddon (1973) 'On the notion of cause, with applications to behaviorism', *Behaviorism* **1**, 25-63.

26. Although we expect to make contact with physiology eventually.

See Staddon, J.E.R. & Bueno, J.L.O. (1991) 'On models, behaviorism and the neural basis of learning', *Psychological Science* **2**, 3-11.

27. See Staddon & Bueno (1991) op. cit.

28. See Staddon & Bueno (1991) op. cit., for a more complete version of this argument.

29. TB takes the Turing-test view of consciousness. This view is not accepted by everyone, however. John Searle (*The rediscovery of the mind*, op. cit.), if I understand him correctly, makes the argument that even if a device were to be found that could pass the Turing test, it would not be conscious. I have three reactions: First, the assumption that such a device can be created solely from hardware may be false, in which case we need say no more. Second is the obvious question, 'How do you know it isn't conscious?' the usual answer to which is 'because it doesn't pass the Turing test.' The third reaction is, 'Wait and see. If such a machine is ever created, people will soon enough treat it as one of their own.' If we are willing to grant consciousness to a dog, or to someone whose ability to communicate is as impaired as Helen Keller's, are we likely to withhold it from a device that speaks and responds indistinguishably from a human being?

30. The theoretical approach to behaviorism is growing and it is hard to single out particular individuals. For surveys see Staddon, J.E.R. (1983) *Learning and adaptive behavior*, Cambridge University Press, Commons, M.L., Grossberg, S. & Staddon, J.E.R. (eds.) (1991) *Neural networks of conditioning and action, the XIIth Harvard Symposium*, Hillsdale, NJ: Erlbaum, Associates. See also theoretical papers by Charles Shimp and Peter Killeen.

31. See Gray, J. (1992) 'Consciousness on the scientific agenda', *Nature* **358**, 277, a report of the Ciba Foundation Symposium 'Experimental and theoretical studies of consciousness'; Crick, F. & Koch, C. (1992) 'The problem of consciousness', *Scientific American*, September, 152-9; Dennett, D.C. & Kinsbourne, M (1992) 'Time and the observer: the where and when of consciousness in the brain', *Behavioral and Brain Sciences* **15**, 183-247.

32. Jeffrey Gray, op. cit., p. 277.

33. Dennett & Kinsbourne, op. cit., p. 186.

34. Op. cit., p. 194.

35. This point is a commonplace in philosophy, but apparently it needs to be reiterated from time to time: 'That different people classify external stimuli in the "same" way does not mean that individual sense qualities are the same for different people (which would be a meaningless statement), but that the systems of sense qualities of different people have a common structure (are homeomorphic systems of relations)' (Hayek, F.A. (1979) *The counterrevolution of science: studies in the abuse of reason*. Indianapolis: Liberty Press [reprint of the 1952 edition], p. 37).

36. Op. cit., p. 187.

37. Dennett & Kinsbourne, op. cit., p. 235.

38. The discreteness is not theoretically necessary, but makes the sequence easier to illustrate.

39. The properties of the states are as yet undefined, of course.

40. It is worth noting that the scientific problem posed by color phi, as I have framed it, parallels exactly the history of research on another perceptual phenomenon: color vision. An early discovery was that people sometimes see 'red' (for example) when no spectrally red light is present – just as people sometimes see movement when nothing is actually moving. Later research expanded on this theme through the study of after-effects, color-contrast and 'Land' effects, eventually showing a wide range of disparities between the color seen and the wavelengths present. The solution to the problem was the discovery of processing mechanisms that define the necessary and sufficient physical-stimulus conditions for a person to report 'green', 'red' or any other color.

41. Popper, K.R. & Eccles, J.C. (1979) *The self and its brain*. Berlin: Springer-Verlag. They write in mystification: 'This antedating procedure does not seem to be explicable by any neurophysiological process … the antedating sensory experience is attributable to the ability of the self-conscious mind to make slight temporal adjustments, i.e. to play tricks with time' (cited in Dennett & Kinsbourne, op. cit., p. 187).

42. No one is immune to cognitive correctness. Jeffrey Gray, op. cit. (1992), in his commentary on the Ciba Foundation Symposium, writes: 'I once asked a radical behaviourist what, in his view, is the difference between two awake individuals, one of them stone deaf, who are both sitting immobile in a room in which a record-player is playing a Mozart string quartet? His answer: their subsequent verbal behavior. Mercifully, there were no radical behaviourists at the symposium.' My response would be 'Do you mean "What do I *know* about the difference?" or "What can I *infer* about it?"' 'What I know' is only the different verbal reports, before and after the experience. 'What I can infer' is something about hearing. Where is the problem?

Index of Names

Index of Names

Subject Index

Subject Index